W9-DJO-559

FLASHMAPS
BOSTON

Editor
Marcy S. Pritchard

Creative Director
Fabrizio La Rocca

Cartographer
David Lindroth

Designer
Tigist Getachew

Editorial Contributors
Robert Blake
Craig Pritchard
Jeff Kennedy

Cartographic Contributors
Edward Faherty
Sheila Levin
Page Lindroth
Eric Rudolph
Gretchen Schmelzer

Contents

Copyright © 1994 by Fodor's Travel Publications, Inc.

Fodor's is a registered trademark of Fodor's Travel Publications, Inc. Flashmaps is a registered trademark of Newberry Award Records, Inc.

Special Sales

Fodor's Travel Publications are available at special discounts for bulk purchases for sales promotions or premiums. Special editions, including personalized covers, excerpts of existing guides, and corporate imprints, can be created in large quantities for special needs. For more information, contact your local bookseller or write to Special Markets, Fodor's Travel Publications, 201 East 50th St., New York, NY 10022. Inquiries from Canada should be directed to your local Canadian bookseller or sent to Random House of Canada, Ltd., Marketing Dept., 1265 Aerowood Dr., Mississauga, Ontario L4W 1B9. Inquiries from the United Kingdom should be sent to Fodor's Travel Publications, 20 Vauxhall Bridge Rd., London, England SW1V 2SA. **ISBN 0-679-02573-1**

MANUFACTURED IN THE UNITED STATES OF AMERICA 10 9 8 7 6 5 4 3 2 1

Area Codes: All (617) unless otherwise noted.

EMERGENCIES

Ambulance/Fire/Police ☎ 911

Animal Rescue League ☎ 426-9170

Animal Shelter (MSPCA)
☎ 522-5055

Animal Emergency ☎ 522-7282

Battered Women ☎ 661-7203

Child Abuse ☎ 800/792-5200

Children's Aid ☎ 267-3700

Coast Guard ☎ 565-9200

Dental Referral ☎ 536-7720

Drug Abuse & Alcohol Helpline
☎ 800/252-6465; 800/873-8732

Poison Information Center
☎ 800/682-9211

Rape Crisis Center ☎ 492-7273

Suicide Prevention ☎ 262-3173

Traveler's Aid ☎ 542-7286

24-Hour Pharmacy
☎ 876-5519; 282-5246

Visiting Nurse Assn ☎ 800/696-3838

SERVICES

AAA ☎ 800/222-4357

AARP ☎ 426-1185

AIDS Hotline ☎ 800/235-2331

Alcoholics Anonymous ☎ 426-9444

Amex Lost Charge Cards
☎ 800/528-4800

Amex Lost Travelers Checks
☎ 800/221-7282

Better Business Bureau ☎ 426-9000

Birth Certificates ☎ 727-7388

**Black Community Information
Center** ☎ 445-3098

Broken Streetlights ☎ 482-5300

Chamber of Commerce ☎ 227-4500

City Hall Boston ☎ 635-4000

City Hall Cambridge ☎ 349-4000

Consumer Affairs ☎ 727-7780

Convention & Visitor's Bureau
☎ 536-4100

Federal Bureau of Investigation
☎ 742-5533

Garbage Collection ☎ 482-5300

Governor's Office ☎ 727-3600

Handicapped Information Center
☎ 727-5540

Immigration ☎ 565-3879

Internal Revenue Service
☎ 536-1040

Legal Advice Center ☎ 742-9179

Library/Boston Public ☎ 536-5400

**Mass Committee Against
Discrimination** ☎ 523-7326

**Mass Turnpike Road/Weather
Conditions** ☎ 800/828-9104

Mayor's Office ☎ 725-4000

Medicare/Medicaid
☎ 800/882-1228

Parking Tickets ☎ 635-4410

Passports ☎ 565-6998

Planned Parenthood ☎ 738-1370

Postal Service ☎ 451-9922

Public Health ☎ 727-2700

Registry of Motor Vehicles
☎ 727-3700

Snow Removal ☎ 482-5300

State Police ☎ 508/820-2300

Time of Day ☎ 637-1234

Towaways ☎ 343-4629

Travel & Tourism ☎ 800/447-6277

Veteran's Administration
☎ 227-4600

Weather ☎ 567-4670

Weather (Marine) ☎ 569-3700

TOURS

Cruises

A C Cruise Line ☎ 261-6633

Bay State Cruise Co ☎ 723-7800

Boston By Sail ☎ 742-3313

Boston Harbor Cruises ☎ 227-4320

Boston Harbor Whale Watch
☎ 345-9866

Charles River Boat Co ☎ 621-3001

Friends of Boston Harbor Islands
☎ 523-8386

Mass Bay Lines ☎ 542-8000

Odyssey Cruises ☎ 654-9700

Spirit of Boston ☎ 569-4449

Sightseeing

Alexander Graham Bell Tour
☎ 743-7691

Bay Colony Historical Tours
☎ 523-7303

Beacon Hill Gardens ☎ 227-4392

Area Codes: All (617) unless otherwise noted.

Beantown Trolley ☎ 986-6100

Boston by Foot ☎ 367-2345

Boston Globe ☎ 929-2653

Boston Public Library ☎ 536-5400

Boston Tours ☎ 899-1454

Boston Trolley ☎ 427-8687

Boston Twilight Mystery Tour
☎ 542-2525

Christian Science Center
☎ 450-3790

Discovering Boston Walking Tour
☎ 323-2554

Federal Reserve Bank ☎ 973-3451

Gray Lines ☎ 426-8805

Historic Boston ☎ 227-4679

Historic Neighborhoods ☎ 426-1885

John Hancock Observatory
☎ 247-1977

Make Way for Ducklings ☎ 426-1885

Mass Bay Brewing Co ☎ 574-9551

Old State House ☎ 242-5642

Old Town Trolley ☎ 269-7010

Skywalk ☎ 236-3118

Trinity Church ☎ 536-0944

Uncommon Boston ☎ 731-5854

USS *Constitution* ☎ 426-1812

Victorian Society ☎ 267-6338

Whites of Their Eyes ☎ 241-7575

TRANSPORTATION

Amtrak ☎ 800/872-7245; 482-3660

Bonanza Bus Terminal ☎ 720-4110

Boston Cab Assn ☎ 536-5010

Ferries

Bay State Cruise Company
Boston to Hull ☎ 723-7800

Hy-Line Ferries
Hyannis to Martha's Vineyard &/or
Nantucket ☎ 508/778-2600

Massachusetts Bay Lines
Boston to Hingham ☎ 542-8000

Steamship Authority
Woods Hole to Martha's Vineyard
☎ 508/693-0367
Hyannis to Nantucket ☎ 508/771-4000

Greyhound ☎ 800/231-2222

**Logan Airport Ground
Transportation** ☎ 800/235-6426

Logan International Airport
☎ 567-5400

Logan Water Shuttle ☎ 330-8680

**Mass Bay Transportation Authority
(MBTA)** ☎ 722-3200; 800/392-6100

MBTA Bus Info ☎ 722-5200

MBTA Commuter Rail ☎ 722-3200;
800/392-6100

**MBTA Hearing Impaired
Information** ☎ 722-5415

MBTA Logan Airport
☎ 800/235-6426

MBTA Lost & Found ☎ 722-5000

MBTA Road Conditions/Weather
☎ 800/828-9104

MBTA Special Needs ☎ 722-5123

Peter Pan Bus Lines ☎ 426-7838

PARKS AND RECREATION

Arnold Arboretum ☎ 524-1717

Beaches ☎ 727-5114

Bicycling ☎ 491-7433

Boating ☎ 523-1038

Fishing ☎ 727-3151

Golf Courses:

George Wright, Hyde Park
☎ 361-8313

William Devine, Dorchester
☎ 265-4084

Fresh Pond, Cambridge ☎ 547-3212

Ponkapoag, Canton ☎ 828-4242

Hiking ☎ 727-0460

Ice Skating ☎ 727-5114

In-Line Skating (rentals) ☎ 482-7400

**Metropolitan District Commission
(MDC)** ☎ 727-5114

Parks & Recreation Info ☎ 635-4505

Racquet Sports ☎ 523-9746

Skiing:

Blue Hills ☎ 828-5070/Downhill

Weston ☎ 891-6575/Cross-country

Swimming ☎ 727-5114

YMCA ☎ 536-7800

YWCA ☎ 536-7940

Boston Athletic Assn ☎ 236-1652
(Marathon)

Area Codes: All (617) unless otherwise noted.

SPECTATOR SPORTS

Boston Bruins/Hockey ☎ 227-3206

Boston Celtics/Basketball ☎ 523-6050

Boston Red Sox/Baseball ☎ 267-8661

New England Patriots/Football ☎ 800/543-1776

Dog Racing/Wonderland ☎ 284-1300

PGA/Pleasant Valley CC ☎ 508/865-4441

LPGA/Blue Hills CC ☎ 828-9725

Horse Racing/Suffolk Downs ☎ 567-3900

Polo/Myopia Hunt Club ☎ 508/468-4433

Tennis/US Pro Longwood ☎ 731-2900

INTERCOLLEGIATE ATHLETICS

Babson ☎ 239-4250

Boston College ☎ 552-3000

Boston University ☎ 353-4632

Brandeis ☎ 736-3630

Harvard ☎ 495-4848

MIT ☎ 253-4498

Northeastern ☎ 437-2672

Tufts ☎ 627-3232

ENTERTAINMENT

Bank of Boston Celebrity Series ☎ 482-2595

Berklee Performance Center ☎ 266-7455

BOSTIX ☎ 723-5181

Boston Ballet ☎ 695-6950

Boston Camerata ☎ 262-2092

Boston Lyric Opera ☎ 248-8811

Boston Opera House ☎ 426-5300

Boston Pops ☎ 266-1492

Boston Symphony Orchestra ☎ 266-2378

Children's Museum ☎ 426-6500

Concertline ☎ 332-9000

Dance Umbrella Inc ☎ 492-7578

Festival Line ☎ 635-3912

Franklin Park Zoo ☎ 442-4896

Great Woods Ctr ☎ 508/339-2333

Handel & Haydn Society ☎ 266-3605

Movie Fone ☎ 333-3456

Museum of Fine Arts ☎ 267-9300

Museum of Science ☎ 723-2500

New England Aquarium ☎ 973-5200

New England Conservatory ☎ 536-2412

Out of Town Tickets ☎ 492-1900

Sanders Theatre/Harvard ☎ 496-2222

Stage Source Line ☎ 423-2475

Symphony Hall ☎ 266-1492

Ticketmaster ☎ 931-2000

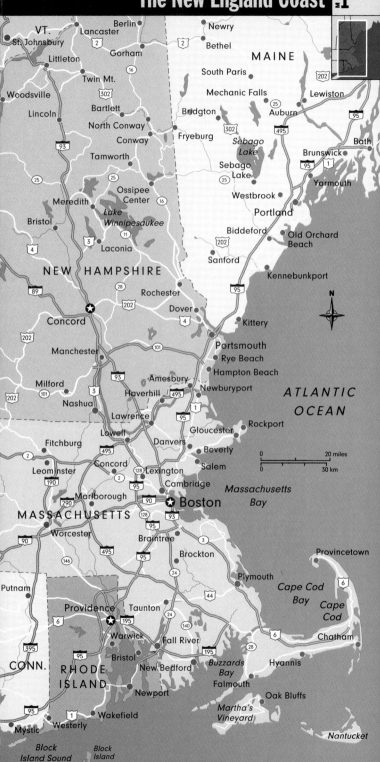

The New England Coast

MAP 1

MAP **2** **Eastern Massachusetts**

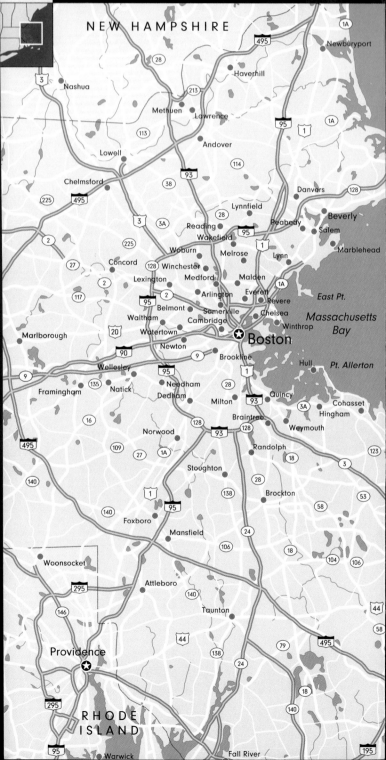

NEW HAMPSHIRE

Newburyport

Nashua

3

28

213

Haverhill

495

1A

Methuen

Lawrence

95

1

113

1A

Andover

Lowell

114

93

Danvers

128

Chelmsford

225

38

495

3

3A

28

Lynnfield

Reading

95

Peabody

Beverly

Salem

Concord

225

Wakefield

Woburn

Melrose

Marblehead

128

Winchester

Medford

Malden

Lynn

1

2

Lexington

117

Arlington

Everett

1A

East Pt.

27

95

2

Belmont

Somerville

Revere

Massachusetts Bay

Waltham

Cambridge

Chelsea

Watertown

Winthrop

Marlborough

20

Newton

Boston

Wellesley

9

Brookline

Hull

Pt. Allerton

90

95

1

9

135

Needham

28

Framingham

Natick

Dedham

Milton

Quincy

16

Milton

93

Cohasset

128

Braintree

3A

Hingham

Norwood

93

128

Weymouth

109

27

1A

Randolph

18

123

140

Stoughton

3

1

28

53

495

140

95

Brockton

58

Foxboro

Mansfield

24

18

104

106

Woonsocket

106

138

Attleboro

295

140

44

146

Taunton

58

Providence

44

79

495

138

24

295

18

RHODE ISLAND

140

95

195

Warwick

Fall River

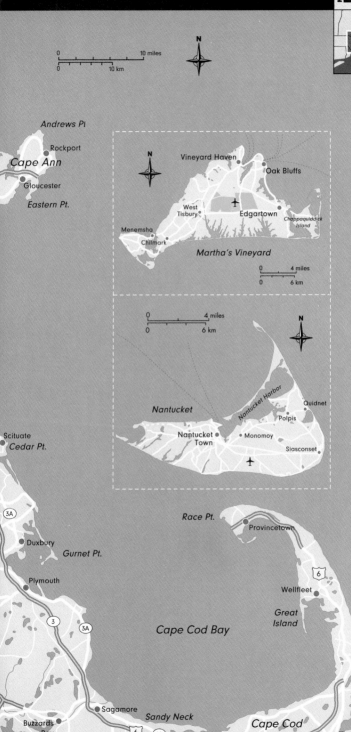

MAP 2

0   10 miles

0   10 km

N

Andrews Pt

Rockport

Cape Ann

Gloucester

Eastern Pt.

N

Vineyard Haven

Oak Bluffs

West Tisbury

Edgartown

Chappaquiddick Island

Menemsha

Chilmark

Martha's Vineyard

0   4 miles

0   6 km

0   4 miles

0   6 km

N

Nantucket

Nantucket Harbor

Quidnet

Polpis

Nantucket Town

Monomoy

Siasconset

Scituate

Cedar Pt.

Race Pt.

Provincetown

Duxbury

Gurnet Pt.

6

Plymouth

Wellfleet

Great Island

3A

Cape Cod Bay

3

3A

Sagamore

Sandy Neck

Cape Cod

Buzzards Bay

28

6

6A

6

28

Hyannis

S. Yarmouth

MAP 3 | **Boston Area**

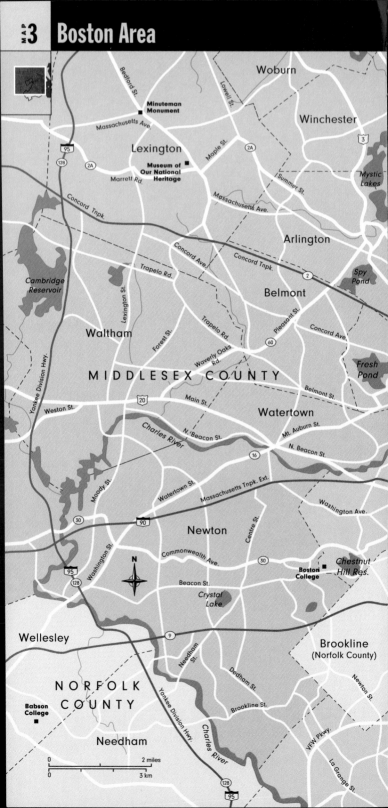

Woburn

Winchester

Minuteman
Monument

Bedford St.

Lowell St.

Massachusetts Ave.

Lexington

Maple St.

Mystic
Lakes

95

128

2A

Museum of
Our National
Heritage

Marrett Rd.

Summer St.

Massachusetts Ave.

Arlington

Concord Tnpk.

Concord Ave.

Concord Tnpk.

2

Spy
Pond

Cambridge
Reservoir

Trapelo Rd.

Belmont

Lexington St.

Pleasant St.

Concord Ave.

Waltham

Forest St.

Trapelo Rd

Waverly Oaks
Rd.

60

Fresh
Pond

MIDDLESEX COUNTY

Yankee Division Hwy.

Belmont St.

Weston St.

20

Main St.

Watertown

Mt. Auburn St.

Charles River

N. Beacon St.

N. Beacon St.

16

Moody St.

Watertown St.

Massachusetts Tnpk. Ext.

Washington Ave.

30

90

Newton

Centre St.

Washington St.

Commonwealth Ave.

30

Boston
College

Chestnut
Hill Res.

N

95

128

Beacon St.

Crystal
Lake

Wellesley

9

Brookline
(Norfolk County)

Needham
St.

Newton St.

**NORFOLK
COUNTY**

Babson
College

Dedham St.

Brookline St.

Yankee Division Hwy.

VFW Pkwy.

La Grange St.

Needham

Charles River

0   2 miles
0   3 km

128

95

3

3

Melrose

Wyoming Ave.

Main St.

Upham St.

Spot Pond

Highland Ave.

Medford

High St.

Malden

Broadway

99

60

Revere

Park Ave.

Broadway

Everett

Revere Beach Pkwy.

Mystic River

Somerville

Broadway

Highland Ave.

Chelsea

107

McClellan Hwy.

Bennington St.

Cambridge

Kirkland St.

Radcliffe College

Harvard University

Prospect St.

Cambridge St.

Northwest Expy.

Northeast Expy.

Mystic River Bridge

Bunker Hill

Msgr. O'Brien Hwy.

1A

Logan International Airport

Broadway

Western Ave.

Massachusetts Ave.

Main St.

Memorial Dr.

MIT

Charles River

North Station

Cambridge St.

Boston University

Starrow Dr.

State House

South Station

Boston Harbor

Commonwealth Ave.

Fenway Park

Prudential Center

Summer St.

D St.

W. Broadway

E. Broadway

Beacon St.

Brookline Ave.

Huntington Ave.

Tremont St.

Washington St.

90

93

1

3

B O S T O N

Jamaica Pond

Columbus Ave.

Warren St.

Dudley St.

Massachusetts Ave.

Dorchester Ave.

Dorchester Bay

Thompson Island

Arnold Arboretum

28

Arbor Way

Columbia Rd.

JFK Library

S U F F O L K   C O U N T Y

Washington St.

Blue Hill Ave.

American Legion Hwy.

Cummins Hwy.

Gallivan Blvd.

28

203

Quincy

3A

MAP 4 — **Streetfinder/Downtown Boston**

A   B   C

Otis St.
Thorndike St.
Spring St.
3rd St.
Lopez Ave.
2nd Hurley St.
1st St.
Charles St.

CAMBRIDGE

Msgr. O'Brien Hwy.
Charlestown Ave.
Lechmere St.

Museum of Science

Rogers St.
Binney St.

Edwin Land Blvd.
Cambridge Pkwy.

Athenaeum St.

N

Charlesbank Park

Nashua

Minot

Martha Rd.
Amy Ct.

WEST END

Blossom Ct.

Wm. Cardinal O'Connell Way

Charles St.
Massachusetts General Hospital
Fruit St.
N Grove St.
Parkman St.
Bridge Ct.
Adams Pl.
Blossom St.

Longfellow Br.

3

Cambridge St. Ave.

Cambridge St.

Garden St.
S. Russell St.
Irving St.
Smith Ct.

3

3

W. Hill Pl.
Charles River Sq.
Revere St.
Pinckney St.

Lindall Pl.
Grove St.
Phillips St.
Primus Ave.
Goodwin Pl.
Anderson St.
Rollins Ct.
Myrtle St.
Louisburg Sq.

Joy St.

BEACON HILL

Mt. Vernon

Walnut St.

Charles River

Hatch Band Shell

Brimmer St.
River St.
W. Cedar St.
Cedar La. Way
Acorn St.
Chestnut St.
Branch St.
Spruce Pl.
Spruce Ct.

Lime St.
Otis Pl.

Beaver Pl.
Byron St.
Beacon St.

4

James J. Storrow Memorial Dr.

Boston Common

Back St.
Beacon St.
Marlborough St.

Dartmouth St.
Berkeley St.

Commonwealth Ave.

Arlington St.

Public Garden

Charles St.

BACK BAY

Townsend Pl.

Boylston St.

5

Newbury St.
Exeter St.
Clarendon St.
Boylston St.
Providence St.
St. James Ave.
Eliot St.
Stuart
Seaver St.

Boston Public Library
Stuart St.

John Hancock Tower

Trinity Pl.

Church St.
Shawmut St.
Piedmont St.
Winchester St.
Broadway
Warren St.
Charles St. S.

Jefferson St.

Edgerly Pl.
Isabella St.
Cortes St.
Melrose St.
Knox St.
Fayette St.
Oak St.

Stanhope St.

PRUDENTIAL CENTER

Blagden St.

Mullin

Prudential Building

90

Back Bay Station

Marginal Rd.

6
9

Huntington Ave.
Harcourt St.

Copley Place

Buckingham St.

28

Cazenove St.
St. Charles St.

Paul Pl.
Herald
Shawmut Ave.
Cobb

St. Botolph St.
Carleton St.
Yarmouth St.
Truro St.
Columbus Ave.
Chandler St.
Lawrence St.
Appleton St.
Gray St.
Tremont St.

SOUTH END

1200 feet
400 meters

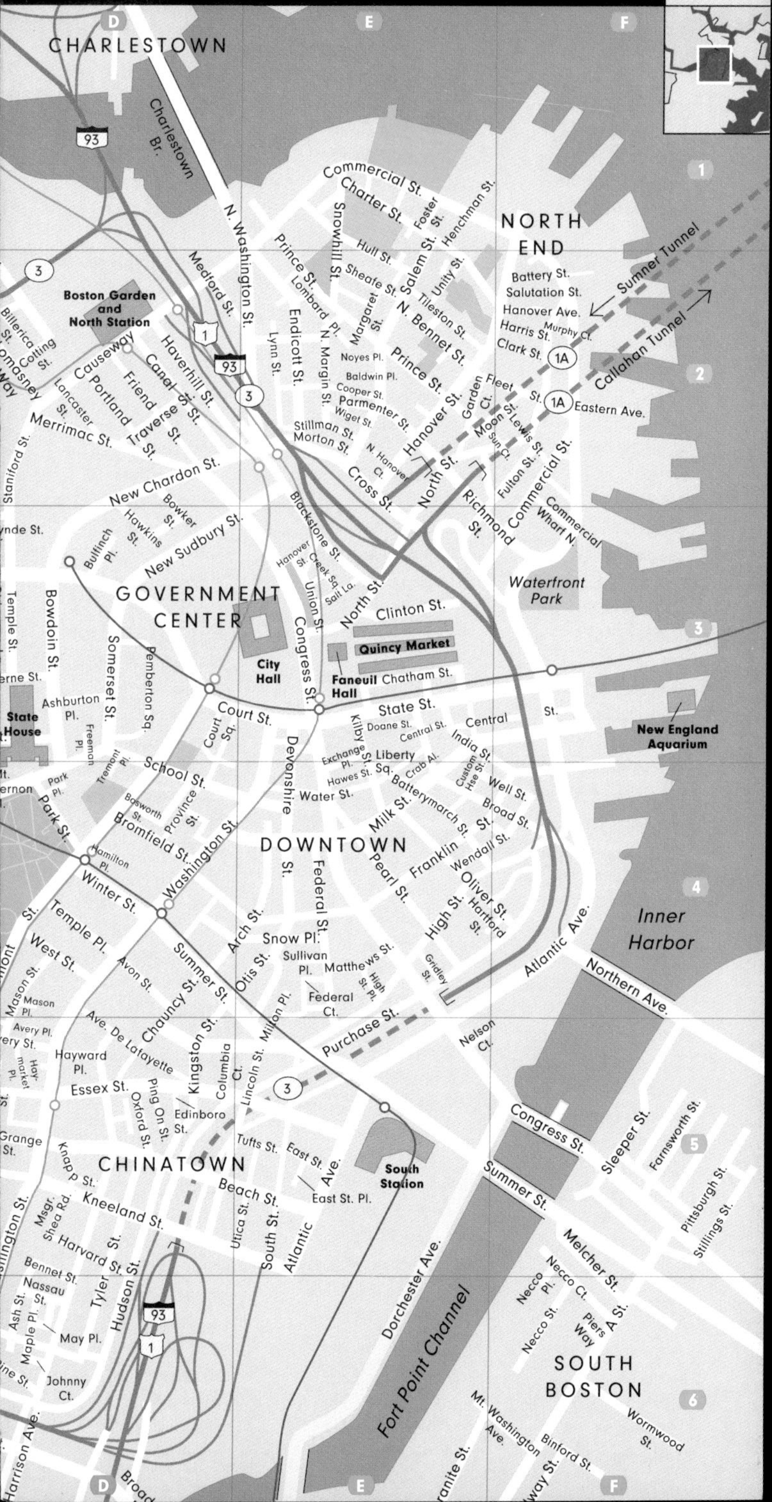

MAP 4

CHARLESTOWN

93

Charlestown Br.

3

N Washington St.

Boston Garden
and North Station

Medford St.

1

93

Causeway St.
Friend St.
Portland St.
Traverse St.

Canal St.
Haverhill St.

Lancaster St.
Merrimac St.

Billerica St.
Cotting St.
Lomasney Way

Lynde St.

Commercial St.

Charter St.

Snowhill St.

Hull St.

Foster St.

Henchman St.

Prince St.

Sheafe St.

Salem St.

Tileston St.

Unity St.

Endicott St.

Lombard Pl.
Cooper St.
Margin St.
Wiget St.

N Bennet St.

Prince St.

Lynn St.

Parmenter St.

Baldwin Pl.

Noyes Pl.

Stillman St.
Morton St.

N Hanover St.

Hanover St.

Cross St.

Blackstone St.

Hanover St.

Creek St.

Canal St.

Salt La.

Union St.

Congress St.

North St.

NORTH
END

Battery St.
Salutation St.
Hanover Ave.
Harris St.
Clark St.

Murphy Ct.

1A

1A

Eastern Ave.

Garden Ct.
Fleet St.
St. Stephen St.

Moon St.

Sun Ct.

Fulton St.

N Hanover Ct.

Richmond
St.

Commercial St.

Commercial Wharf N.

Sumner Tunnel

Callahan Tunnel

Waterfront
Park

GOVERNMENT
CENTER

New Chardon St.

Bowker St.

Hawkins St.

New Sudbury St.

Buttinch Pl.

Temple St.

Bowdoin St.

Somerset St.

Pemberton Sq.

City
Hall

Clinton St.

Quincy Market

Faneuil
Hall

Chatham St.

New England
Aquarium

Ashburton
Pl.

State
House

Freeman
Pl.

Court St.

Court
Sq.

Devonshire St.

State St.

Doane St.

Central St.

Central

St.

India St.

School St.

Bosworth St.

Province St.

Washington St.

Bromfield St.

Hamilton Pl.

Winter St.

Exchange
Pl.

Kilby St.

Liberty
Sq.

Hawes St.

Water St.

Milk St.

Batterymarch St.

Crab Al.

Well St.

Broad St.

Custom
House

DOWNTOWN

Federal St.

Pearl St.

Franklin St.

Wendall St.

Oliver St.

High St.

Hartford
St.

Inner
Harbor

Park St.

Vernon St.

Temple Pl.

West St.

Avon St.

Arch St.

Chauncy St.

Summer St.

Snow Pl.

Sullivan
Pl.

Matthews St.

Godfrey
St.

Atlantic Ave.

Northern Ave.

Mason St.
Avery Pl.
Avery St.

Hayward
Pl.

Ave De Lafayette

Federal
Ct.

Purchase St.

Nelson
Ct.

Hay-
market

Essex St.

Kingston St.

Columbia St.

Lincoln St.

Milan St.

3

Congress St.

Sleeper St.

Farnsworth St.

Grange
St.

CHINATOWN

Knapp St.

Kneeland St.

Beach St.

Ping On St.
Oxford St.

Edinboro
St.

Tufts St.

East St.

East St. Pl.

South
Station

Summer St.

Melcher St.

Pittsburgh St.
Stillings St.

Magr.
Shea Rd.

Harvard St.

Utica St.

South St.

Atlantic

Ave.

Dorchester Ave.

Necco St.
Necco Ct.
Piers A
St.

Necco
Pl.

Necco
Way

Bennet St.
Nassau St.

Tyler St.

Hudson St.

93

1

Ash St.
Maple Pl.

May Pl.

Johnny
Ct.

Fort Point Channel

SOUTH
BOSTON

Mt. Washington
Ave.

Binford St.

Wormwood
St.

MAP 4

Streetfinder/Downtown Boston

Letter codes refer to grid sectors on preceding map

A St. E6, F5
Acorn St. C4
Adams Pl. C3
Amy Ct. C2
Anderson St. C3
Appleton St. A6, C6
Arch St. D4, E4
Arlington St. B4, C6
Ash St. D5, D6
Ashburton Pl. D3
Atlantic Ave. E5, F2
Ave. De Lafayette D4, D5
Avery Pl. D5
Avery St. D5
Avon St. D4
Back St. A5, B4
Baldwin Pl. E2
Battery St. F2
Batterymarch St. E4
Beach St. D5, E5
Beacon St. A5, D3
Beaver Pl. B4
Bennet St. D5, D6
Berkeley St. B4, B6
Billerica St. D2
Binford St. F6
Blackstone St. D2, E3
Blagden St. A5, A6
Blossom Ct. C2
Blossom St. C2, C3
Bosworth St. D4
Bowdoin St. D3
Bowker St. D2, D3
Boylston Pl. C5
Boylston St. A6, C5
Branch St. C4
Bridge Ct. C3
Brimmer St. B3, B4
Broad St. E4, F4
Broadway Bridge D6
Broadway C5, C6
Bromfield St. D4
Buckingham St. B6
Bulfinch Pl. D3
Byron St. B4, C4
Callahan Tunnel E2, F1
Cambridge St. Ave. B3, C3
Cambridge St. B3, D3
Canal St. D2
Carleton St. A6
Causeway D2, E1
Cazenove St. B6

Cedar Lane Way B3, C4
Central St. E3, F3
Chandler St. B6, C6
Charles River Sq. B3
Charles St. C2, C5
Charles St. S. C5, C6
Charlestown Bridge D1
Charter St. E1, E2
Chatham St. E3
Chauncy St. D4, D5
Chestnut St. B4, C4
Church St. C5, C6
Clarendon St. A4, B6
Clark St. F2
Clinton St. E3
Cobb St. C6
Columbia Ct. D5
Columbus Ave. A6, C5
Commercial St. E1, E3
Commercial Wharf N. F2, F3
Commonwealth Ave. A5, B4
Congress St. E3, F6
Cooper St. E2
Cortes St. B6, C6
Cotting St. D2
Court Sq. D3, D4
Court St. D3, E3
Crab Al. E4
Creek Sq. E3
Cross St. E2, E3
Custom House St. E4
Dartmouth St. A4, B6
Derne St. D3
Devonshire St. E3, E4
Doane St. E3
Dorchester Ave. E6, F4
East St. E5
East St. Pl. E5
Eastern Ave. F2
Edgerly Pl. C5, C6
Edinboro St. D5
Endicott St. E2
Essex St. C5, E5
Exchange Pl. E3, E4
Exeter St. A5, A6
Farnsworth St. F5
Fayette St. C5, C6
Federal Ct. E4
Federal St. E4, E5
Fleet St. E2, F2
Foster St. E1

Franklin St. D4, F4
Freeman Pl. D3
Friend St. D2
Fruit St. B2, C2
Fulton St. E2, F2
Garden Ct. E2
Garden St. C3
Garrison St. A6
Goodwin Pl. C3
Granite St. E6
Gray St. B6
Gridley St. E4
Grove St. C3
Hamilton Pl. D4
Hancock St. C3, D3
Hanover Ave. F2
Hanover St. E3, F1
Harcourt St. A6
Harris St. F2
Harrison Ave. C6, D5
Hartford St. E4, F4
Harvard St. D5
Haverhill St. D2, E2
Hawes St. E4
Hawkins St. D3
Haymarket Pl. D5
Hayward Pl. D5
Henchman St. E1
Herald St. C6, D6
High St. E5, F4
High St. Pl. E4
Hudson St. D5, D6
Hull St. E1, E2
Huntington Ave. A6
India St. E3, F4
Irving St. C3
Isabella St. B6, C6
James J. Storrow Memorial Dr. A4, B4
Jefferson St. C6
Johnny Ct. D6
Joy Pl. C4, D4
Joy St. C3, C4
Kilby St. E3, E4
Kingston St. D4, D5
Knapp St. D5
Kneeland St. D5, E5
LaGrange St. C5, D5
Lancaster St. D2
Lawrence St. B6
Lewis St. F2
Liberty Sq. E4
Lincoln St. D5, E5

MAP 4

Letter codes refer to grid sectors on preceding map

MAP 5 Streetfinder/Cambridge

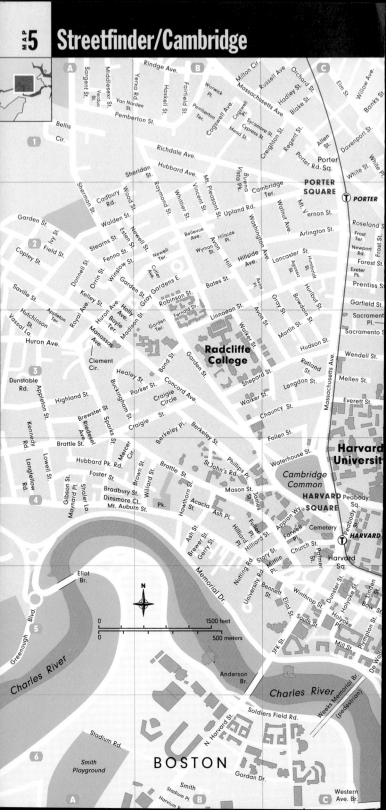

MAP 5

D   E   F

1

SPRING HILL

SOMERVILLE

2

3

Conway
Plgd.

Dickerman
Plgd.

Lincoln
Pk.

INMAN SQUARE
Inman
Sq.

4

5

CENTRAL SQUARE

CENTRAL Ⓣ
Central
Sq.

6

Hoyt
Field

Woodbine St.
Albion St.
Hudson St.
Highland Ave.
Crocker St.
Tower St.
Lowell St.
Crown St.
Braslow Ave.
Springhill Ter.
Central St.
Waldo St.
Richdale Ave.
Montrose Ave.
Madison Ave.
Sycamore St.
Hancock St.
Cherry St.
Cedar St.
Cedar Ave.
Porter Ave.
Summer St.
Cedar Ave.
Gibbens St.
Cambria St.
Oxford St.
Berkeley St.
Hersey St.
Highland Ave.
Elm St.
Holyoke Rd.
Cedar Pl.
Olive Ave.
Gussie Ter.
Gove Ct.
Linden Ave.
Porter St.
Craigie Ter.
Lowell Cir.
Belmont St.
Westwood Rd.
Benton Rd.
Summer St.
Carter Ter.
Avon St.
Mossland
Somerville Ave.
Oak Ter.
Kimball St.
Ibbetson St.
Lowell St.
Belmont Pl.
Belmont Ter.
Spring St.
Monmouth St.
Elm Pl.
Harvard St.
Cleveland St.
Laurel St.
Central St.
Preston Rd.
Quincy St.
Prescott St.
Oxford St.
Traymore St.
Stanford Ter.
Harris St.
Miller St.
Eustis St.
Crescent St.
Sacramento St.
Carver St.
Howland St.
Beacon St.
Kent St.
Garden Ct.
Kent Ct.
Bleachery Ct.
Allen Ct.
Park Pl.
Loring St.
Granite St.
Knapp St.
School St.
Summer St.
Bow Pl.
Hammond St.
Francis Ave.
Museum St.
Harrison St.
Ivaloo St.
Tower Ct.
Timmins Pl.
Tyler St.
Somerville Ave.
Church St.
Lake St.
Bow St.
Kilby St.
Bryant St.
Morgan St.
Park St.
Vine Ct.
Village St.
Dane Ave.
Leland St.
Perry St.
Parker St.
Arnold Ct.
Eliot St.
Hanson St.
Dane St.
Rose St.
Parkdale St.
Bowdoin St.
Shady Hill Sq.
Skehan St.
Durham St.
Lewis St.
Holden Ct.
Scott St.
Sedgwick St.
Farrar St.
Washington St.
Beacon St.
Magnus Ave.
Lincoln Pkwy.
Irving St.
Myrtle Ave.
Beacon St.
Smith Ave.
Calvin St.
Marion St.
Adrian St.
Kirkland Pl.
Frisbie Pl.
Divinity Ave.
Kirkland St.
Magnolia Ave.
Waldo Ave.
Dimick St.
Harold St.
Concord Ave.
Wyatt St.
Springfield St.
Oak St.
Holts Ave.
Houghton St.
Ashton Pl.
Irving Ter.
Trowbridge St.
Baldwin Ct.
Adams Ter.
Roberts Rd.
Hovey Ave.
Leonard Ave.
Camelia Ave.
Line St.
Cooney St.
Hammond St.
Dickinson St.
Oakland St.
Clary St.
Cambridge St.
Cambridge St.
Marie Ave.
Inman St.
Fainwood Cir.
Hampshire St.
Carlisle St.
Oxford St.
Oak St.
Quincy St.
Prescott St.
Fenton St.
Ellery St.
Dana St.
Ellsworth Ave.
Highland Ave.
Maple Ave.
Fayette St.
Antrim St.
Amory St.
Gardner Rd.
Murdock St.
Broadway
Trowbridge Pl.
Cleveland St.
Merrill St.
Chatham St.
Fayette Pk.
Corliss Pl.
Inman St.
St. Mary Rd.
King Pl.
Amory Pl.
Broadway
Tremont St.
Norfolk St.
Elm St.
Arrow St.
Mt. Auburn St.
Remington St.
Trowbridge Pl.
Ellery St.
Harvard St.
Dana St.
Centre St.
Hancock St.
Lee St.
Clinton St.
Inman Pl.
West St.
West Pl.
Prospect St.
Conant St.
Athens St.
Banks St.
Grant St.
Surrey St.
Pewter
Green St.
Franklin St.
Boy St.
Belvidere St.
Cottage Row
Massachusetts Ave.
Bigelow St.
Inman St.
St. Paul St.
Essex St.
Norfolk Ct.
Richardson St.
Columbia St.
Fallon Pl.
Flagg St.
Putnam St.
Kinnaird St.
Hayes St.
Howard St.
Magee St.
Joy St.
Soden St.
Franklin St.
Pleasant St.
Austin Pk.
Essex Pl.
Temple St.
Worcester St.
Suffolk St.
Pine St.
Walker St.
Walker Ct.
Hewes St.
Elmer St.
Akron St.
Callender St.
Dodge St.
Jay St.
Jay Pl.
Soden Pl.
Western Ave.
Central Pl.
Temple St.
Vail Ct.
Bishop Allen Dr.
Washington St.
Douglass St.
Eaton St.
Medford St.
Dodge St.
River St.
Magazine St.

MAP 5

Streetfinder/Cambridge

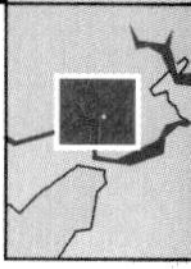

Letter codes refer to grid sectors on preceding map

MAP **6** **Zip Codes**

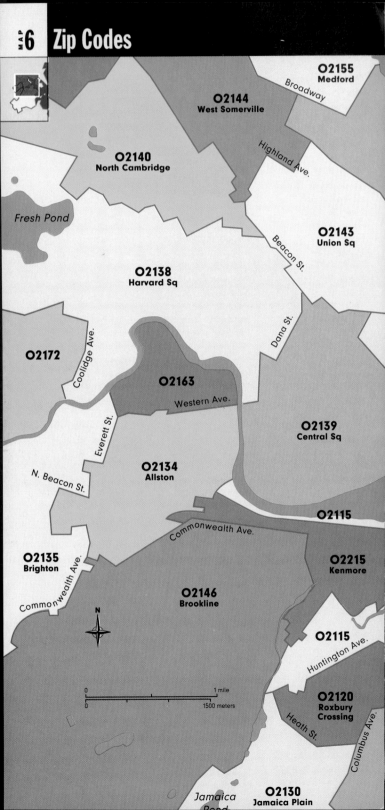

O2155 Medford

Broadway

O2144 West Somerville

Highland Ave.

O2140 North Cambridge

Fresh Pond

Beacon St.

O2143 Union Sq

O2138 Harvard Sq

Dana St.

Coolidge Ave.

O2172

O2163

Western Ave.

Everett St.

O2139 Central Sq

O2134 Allston

N. Beacon St.

Commonwealth Ave.

O2115

O2135 Brighton

Commonwealth Ave.

O2215 Kenmore

O2146 Brookline

N

O2115

Huntington Ave.

O2120 Roxbury Crossing

Heath St.

Columbus Ave.

0   1 mile
0   1500 meters

Jamaica Pond

O2130 Jamaica Plain

MAP **6**

O2149
Everett

O2150
Chelsea

O2145
Winter Hill

Mystic River

Medford St.

O2129
Charlestown

O2128
East Boston

O2141
East Cambridge

Rogers St.

O2114
West End

O2109

O2113
Hanover St

O2142
Kendall Sq

O2202
State Offices

O2203
JFK Bldg

O2201
City Hall

Charles River

O2133
State House

O2109

*Boston
Inner
Harbor*

O2108

O2110

J.W. McCormack PO
02101–02107
02208, 02209

O2116
Back Bay

Mass. Ave.

Boylston St.

O2117

O2111

O2210

O2199
Prudential Ctr

O2115

O2118
South End

O2127
South Boston

Massachusetts Ave.

O2119
Roxbury

Cottage St.

O2125
Dorchester

Old Harbor

MAP 7 Neighborhoods

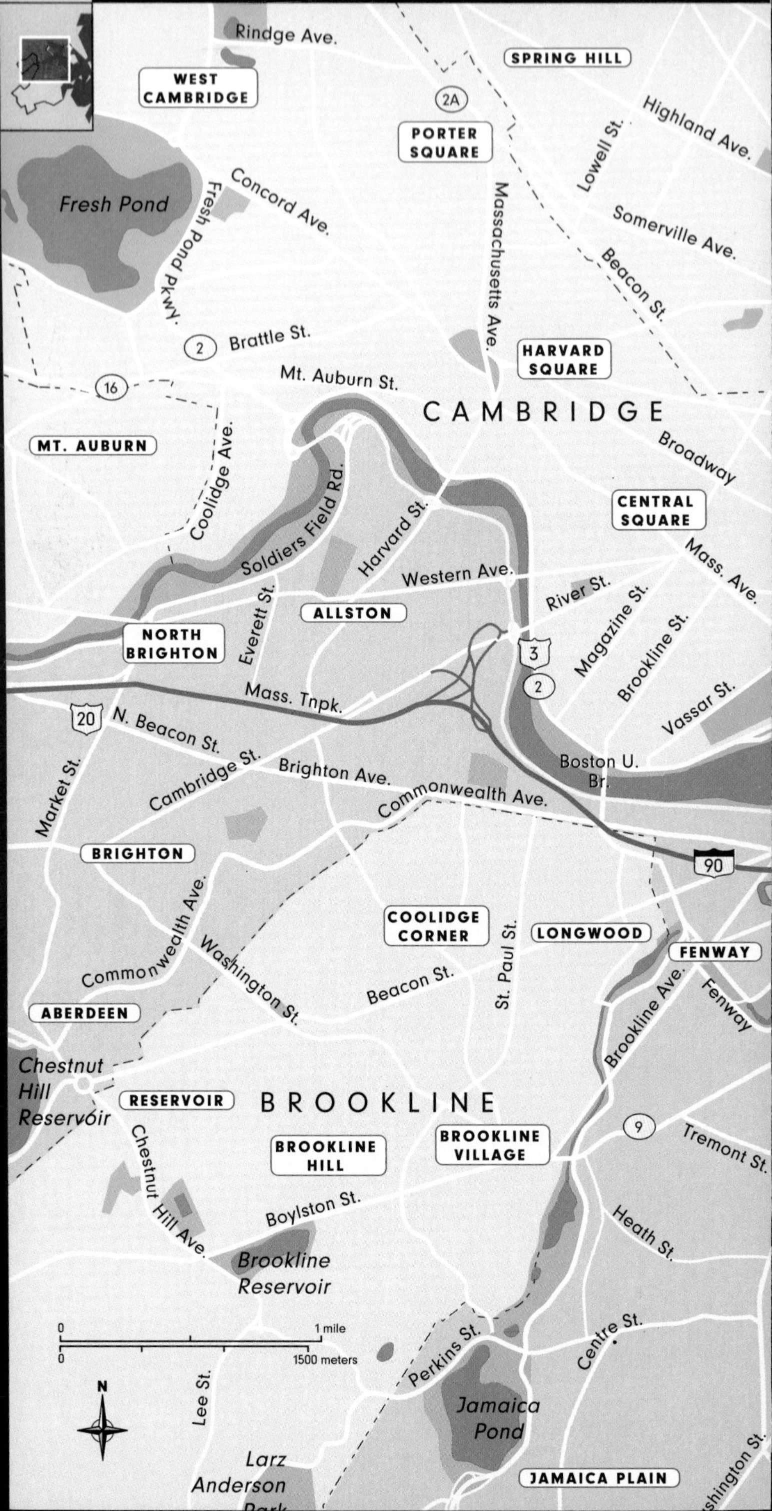

Rindge Ave.

SPRING HILL

WEST CAMBRIDGE

2A

PORTER SQUARE

Fresh Pond

Concord Ave.

Lowell St.

Highland Ave.

Fresh Pond Pkwy.

Somerville Ave.

Massachusetts Ave.

Beacon St.

2 Brattle St.

HARVARD SQUARE

Mt. Auburn St.

16

C A M B R I D G E

MT. AUBURN

Coolidge Ave.

Broadway

CENTRAL SQUARE

Soldiers Field Rd.

Harvard St.

Western Ave.

Mass. Ave.

ALLSTON

River St.

Magazine St.

Brookline St.

3

NORTH BRIGHTON

Everett St.

Mass. Tnpk.

2

Vassar St.

20 N. Beacon St.

Boston U. Br.

Market St.

Cambridge St.

Brighton Ave.

Commonwealth Ave.

90

BRIGHTON

Washington Ave.

COOLIDGE CORNER

St. Paul St.

LONGWOOD

FENWAY

Commonwealth Ave.

Beacon St.

Brookline Ave.

Fenway

ABERDEEN

Chestnut Hill Reservoir

RESERVOIR

B R O O K L I N E

9

Tremont St.

Chestnut Hill Ave.

BROOKLINE HILL

BROOKLINE VILLAGE

Boylston St.

Heath St.

Brookline Reservoir

| 0 | | 1 mile |
| 0 | | 1500 meters |

Lee St.

N

Perkins St.

Centre St.

Jamaica Pond

Larz Anderson Park

JAMAICA PLAIN

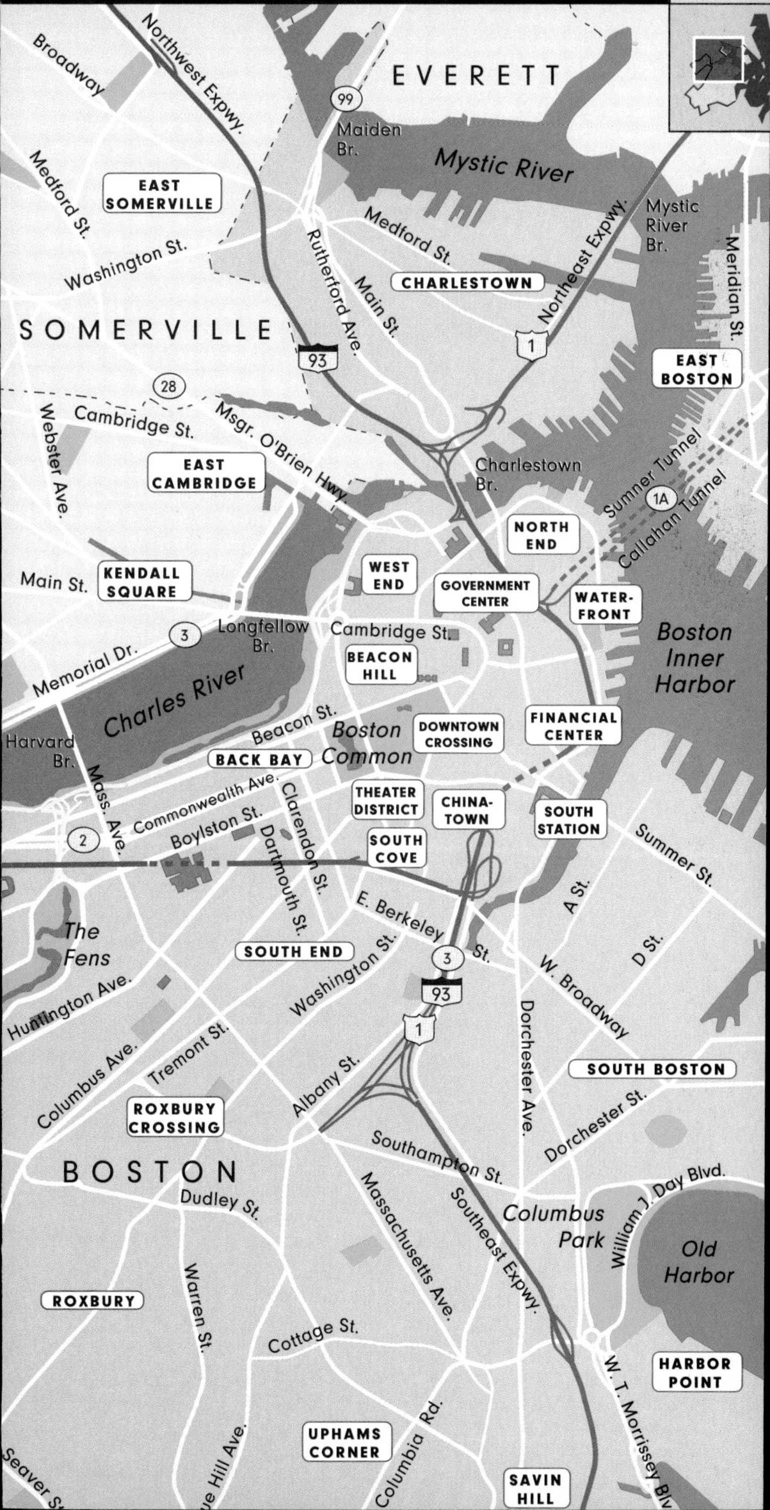

MAP 7

EVERETT

Broadway

Northwest Expwy.

99

Maiden Br.

Mystic River

Medford St.

EAST SOMERVILLE

Washington St.

Medford St.

Rutherford Ave.

CHARLESTOWN

Northeast Expwy.

Mystic River Br.

1

SOMERVILLE

Main St.

93

Meridian St.

EAST BOSTON

28

Cambridge St.

Msgr. O'Brien Hwy.

Webster Ave.

EAST CAMBRIDGE

Charlestown Br.

Sumner Tunnel

1A

Callahan Tunnel

Main St.

KENDALL SQUARE

NORTH END

GOVERNMENT CENTER

WEST END

WATER-FRONT

Boston Inner Harbor

Longfellow Br.

3

Memorial Dr.

Cambridge St.

BEACON HILL

Charles River

Harvard Br.

Beacon St.

Boston Common

DOWNTOWN CROSSING

FINANCIAL CENTER

BACK BAY

Mass. Ave.

Commonwealth Ave.

2

THEATER DISTRICT

CHINA-TOWN

SOUTH STATION

Boylston St.

Clarendon St.

Dartmouth St.

SOUTH COVE

Summer St.

E. Berkeley St.

A St.

D St.

SOUTH END

Washington St.

3

W. Broadway

The Fens

Huntington Ave.

Columbus Ave.

Tremont St.

93

1

Dorchester Ave.

SOUTH BOSTON

Dorchester St.

ROXBURY CROSSING

Albany St.

Southampton St.

BOSTON

Dudley St.

Massachusetts Ave.

Southeast Expwy.

Columbus Park

William J. Day Blvd.

Old Harbor

ROXBURY

Warren St.

Columbia Rd.

Cottage St.

W. T. Morrissey Blvd.

HARBOR POINT

Seaver St.

UPHAMS CORNER

SAVIN HILL

MAP 8 **Hospitals/Boston Area**

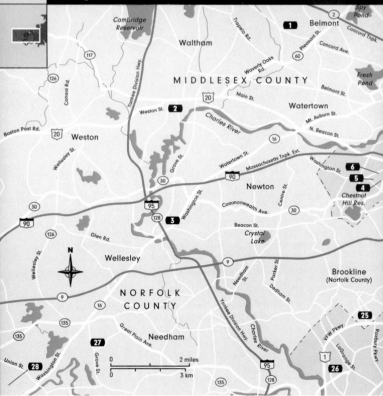

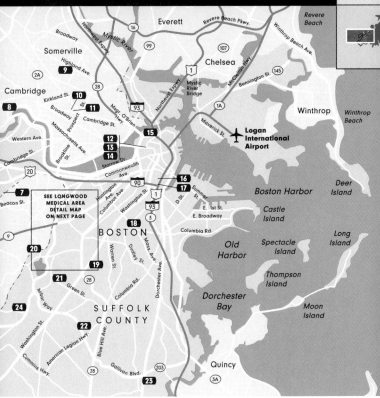

MAP 8

Everett

Broadway

Somerville

Highland Ave.

Cambridge

Kirkland St.

Broadway

Cambridge St.

Western Ave.

Massachusetts Ave.

Cambridge St.

Beacon St.

SEE LONGWOOD
MEDICAL AREA
DETAIL MAP
ON NEXT PAGE

BOSTON

Huntington Ave.
Columbus Ave.

Washington St.

Commonwealth Ave.

Mass. Ave.

Warren St.

Dudley St.

Green St.

Columbia Rd.

Dorchester Ave.

SUFFOLK
COUNTY

Arbor Way

Washington St.

American Legion Hwy.

Cummins Hwy.

Blue Hill Ave.

Gallivan Blvd.

Mystic River

Northwest Expwy.

Magr. O'Brien Hwy.

Northeast Expwy.

Mystic
River
Bridge

Storrow Dr.

Revere Beach Pkwy.

Chelsea

Bennington St.

McClellan Hwy.

Maverick St.

Winthrop Beach Ave.

Revere
Beach

Winthrop

Winthrop
Beach

Logan
International
Airport

Boston Harbor

Deer
Island

Castle
Island

Summer St.

D St.

E. 1st St.

E. Broadway

Columbia Rd.

Old
Harbor

Spectacle
Island

Long
Island

Thompson
Island

Dorchester
Bay

Moon
Island

Quincy

Listed by Site Number (cont.)

15 Spaulding Rehab
16 Univ-BU Med Center
17 New Eng Medical Center
18 Boston City
19 Jewish Memorial
20 Brookline
21 Arbour Psychiatric
22 Lemuel Shattuck
23 Carney
24 Faulkner
25 Bournewood
26 VA-Med Center
27 Charles River
28 Leonard Morse

Listed Alphabetically (cont.)

McLean, 1. 115 Mill St, Belmont
☎ 855-2000

Mt Auburn, 8. 330 Mt Auburn St,
Cambridge ☎ 492-3500

New Eng Med Center, 17.
750 Washington St ☎ 956-5000

Newton-Wellesley, 3. 2014 Washington
St, Newton ☎ 243-6000

St Elizabeth's, 5. 736 Cambridge St,
Brighton ☎ 789-3000

St John of God, 7. 296 Allston St,
Brighton ☎ 277-5750

Shriner's Hospital, 14. 51 Blossom St
☎ 722-3000

Somerville, 9. 230 Highland Ave,
Somerville ☎ 666-4400

Spaulding Rehabilitation, 15.
125 Nashua St ☎ 720-6400

Univ-BU Med Center, 16.
88 E Newton St ☎ 638-8000

VA-Med Center, 26. 1400 VFW Pkwy,
W Roxbury ☎ 323-7700

Waltham-Weston, 2. Hope Ave,
Waltham ☎ 647-6000

Youville, 10. 1575 Cambridge St,
Cambridge ☎ 876-4344

MAP 9

Hospitals/Longwood Medical Area

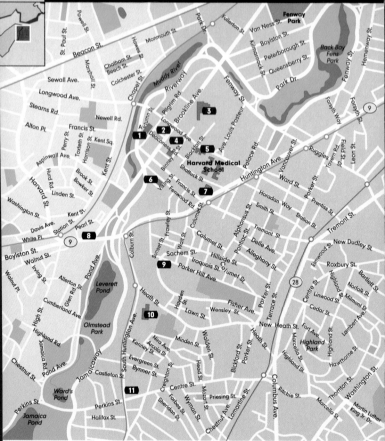

Listed by Site Number

1 New England
   Deaconess

2 Joslin Diabetes
   Center

3 Beth Israel

4 Children's

5 Dana-Farber Cancer
   Institute

6 Mass Mental Health
   Center

7 Brigham & Women's

8 Brookline Animal
   Hospital

9 New England Baptist

10 VA-Med Ctr

11 Angell Memorial
   Animal Hospital

Listed Alphabetically

**Angell Memorial Animal
Hospital, 11.** 350 So Huntington Ave,
☎ 522-7282

Beth Israel, 3. 330 Brookline Ave
☎ 735-2000

Brigham & Women's, 7. 75 Francis St
☎ 732-5500

Brookline Animal Hospital, 8.
678 Brookline Ave ☎ 232-9500

Children's, 4. 300 Longwood Ave
☎ 735-6000

Dana-Farber Cancer Inst, 5.
44 Binney St ☎ 632-3000

Joslin Diabetes Ctr, 2. 1 Joslin Pl
☎ 732-2400

Mass Mental Health Ctr, 6.
74 Fenwood Rd ☎ 734-1300

New Eng Baptist, 9. 91 Parker Hill
Ave ☎ 738-5800

New Eng Deaconess, 1. 185 Pilgrim Rd
☎ 732-7000

VA-Med Ctr, 10. 150 So Huntington
Ave, Jamaica Plain ☎ 232-9500

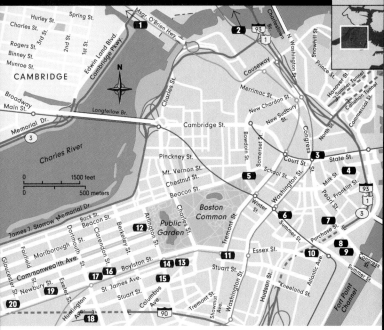

Listed Alphabetically

Australia, 5. 20 Beacon St
☎ 248-8655

Austria, 7. 211 Congress St
☎ 426-0330

Belgium, 2. 300 Commercial St,
Malden ☎ 397-8566

Canada, 18. 3 Copley Pl ☎ 262-3760

Cape Verde, 16. 535 Boylston St
☎ 353-0014

Chile, 4. 79 Milk St ☎ 426-1678

Colombia, 16. 535 Boylston St
☎ 536-6222

Denmark, 17. 545 Boylston St
☎ 266-8418

Dominican Rep, 14. 20 Park Plaza
☎ 482-8121

Ecuador, 3. 60 State St ☎ 227-7200

Finland, 6. 101 Arch St ☎ 951-0009

France, 12. 3 Commonwealth Ave
☎ 266-1680

Germany, 16. 535 Boylston St
☎ 536-4414

Great Britain, 8. 600 Atlantic Ave
☎ 248-9555

Greece, 14. 20 Park Plaza
☎ 542-3240

Haiti, 17. 545 Boylston St ☎ 266-3660

Ireland, 16. 535 Boylston St
☎ 267-9330

Israel, 13. 20 Park Pl

Italy, 11. 100 Boylston St ☎ 542-0483

Japan, 9. Federal Reserve Plaza
☎ 973-9772

Mexico, 14. 20 Park Plaza
☎ 426-4942

Monaco, 1. 251 Payston Rd, Belmont
☎ 489-1240

Netherlands, 15. 6 St James Ave
☎ 542-8452

Pakistan, 19. 745 Boylston St
☎ 267-5555

Peru, 16. 535 Boylston St ☎ 267-4050

Portugal, 20. 899 Boylston St
☎ 536-8740

Republic of Korea, 10.
One Financial Ctr ☎ 348-3660

Spain, 17. 545 Boylston St
☎ 536-2506

Sweden, 15. 6 St James Ave
☎ 426-5558

Switzerland, 16. 535 Boylston St
☎ 266-2038

Venezuela, 17. 545 Boylston St
☎ 266-9368

MAP 11 **Libraries/Greater Boston**

Fresh Pond
Huron Ave.
Concord Ave.
Somerville Ave.
Union Sq.
School St.
Belmont St.
Arlington St.
Huron Ave.
Aberdeen Ave.
Fresh Pond Pkwy.
Brattle St.
Mt. Auburn St.
Harvard Sq.
Kirkland St.
Prospect St.
Washington St.
28
1
Harvard University
Broadway
Hampshire St.
Mt. Auburn St.
Mt. Auburn Cemetery
Grove St.
Harvard St.
Central Sq.
Massachusetts Ave.
Main St.
16
WATERTOWN
Arsenal St.
Soldiers Field Rd.
N. Harvard St.
JFK Dr.
Western Ave.
River St.
Magazine St.
Brookline St.
CAMBRIDGE
MI
20
ALLSTON
Briggs Field (MIT)
90
20
N. Beacon St.
3
2
Harvard Br.
Market St.
Cambridge St.
Harvard Ave.
Brighton Ave.
Commonwealth Ave.
Boston U. Br.
Storrow Dr.
90
6
4
Ringer Park
Washington St.
5
Gallagher Memorial Park
Chandler Pond
BRIGHTON
ABERDEEN
Commonwealth Ave.
COOLIDGE CORNER
Harvard St.
Beacon St.
7
90
The Fens
Lake St.
Chestnut Hill Ave.
Commonwealth Ave.
Beacon St.
8
9
Beacon St.
Cleveland Circle
Chestnut Hill Res.
Huntington Ave.
9
10
B
CHESTNUT HILL
BROOKLINE HILL
Brookline Reservoir
Columbus Ave.
Hammond Pond Pkwy.
Hammond's Pond
Boylston St.
BROOKLINE
BROOKLINE VILLAGE
Olmstead Park
Centre St.
9
Holyhood Cemetery
Perkins St.
14
28
Lee St.
Jamaica Pond
Centre St.
15
Seaver St.
Brookline St.
Brookline Golf Course
Larz Anderson Park
Centre St.
JAMAICA PLAIN
Washington St.
Newton St.
Walnut Hill Cemetery
16
17
South St.
Franklin Park
WESTBROOK VILLAGE
St. Joseph's Cemetery
Mt. Benedict Cemetery
Veterans of Foreign Wars Pkwy.
Arnold Arboretum
FOREST HILLS
Morton St.
Walk Hill St.
Forest Hills Cemetery
Baker St. Cemetery
Corey St.
West Roxbury Pkwy.
Centre St.
ROSLINDALE
Fallon Field
Washington St.
American Legion Hwy.
Blue Hill
HIGHLAND
23
BELLEVUE
Belgrade Ave.
MT HOPE
24
Cummins Hwy.
Mt. Hope Cemetery
25
Lagrange St.
Beech St.
26
MATTAPAN

Listed by Site Number

1 Smithsonian Astrophysical	**6** Zion Research	**12** Washington Village
2 East Boston	**7** Art Institute Boston	**13** South Boston
3 Orient Heights	**8** Temple Israel	**14** Connolly
4 Faneuil	**9** Museum of Fine Arts	**15** Egleston Square
5 Brighton	**10** Parker Hill	**16** Arnold Arboretum
	11 Dudley	

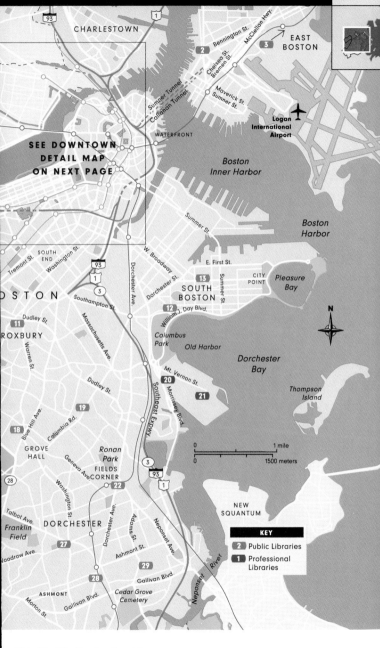

MAP 11

CHARLESTOWN

EAST BOSTON

Bennington St.

McClellan Hwy.

Chelsea St.
Bremen St.

Sumner Tunnel
Callahan Tunnel

Maverick St.
Sumner St.

WATERFRONT

Logan
International
Airport

SEE DOWNTOWN
DETAIL MAP
ON NEXT PAGE

Boston
Inner Harbor

Boston
Harbor

Summer St.

SOUTH
END

Tremont St.

Washington St.

W. Broadway

Dorchester St.

E. First St.

CITY
POINT

Pleasure
Bay

SOUTH
BOSTON

Dorchester Ave.

Summer St.

BOSTON

Southampton St.

Dudley St.

William J. Day Blvd.

Columbus
Park

Old Harbor

Dorchester
Bay

ROXBURY

Warren St.

Massachusetts Ave.

Dudley St.

Mt. Vernon St.

Morrissey Blvd.

Thompson
Island

Blue Hill Ave.

Columbia Rd.

Southeast Expwy.

GROVE
HALL

Geneva Ave.

Ronan
Park

FIELDS
CORNER

Washington St.

DORCHESTER

Dorchester Ave.

Adams St.

Ashmont St.

Neponset Ave.

Talbot Ave.

Franklin
Field

Woodrow Ave.

ASHMONT

Morton St.

Gallivan Blvd.

Gallivan Blvd.

Cedar Grove
Cemetery

Neponset River

NEW
SQUANTUM

0   1 mile
0   1500 meters

KEY
Public Libraries
Professional
Libraries

Listed by Site Number (cont.)

MAP 11 Libraries/Downtown

KEY

37	Public Libraries
38	Professional Libraries

Listed Alphabetically
PUBLIC

Adams St, 29. 690 Adams St, Dorchester ☎ 436-6900

Boston Public, 46. 666 Boylston St ☎ 536-5400

Brighton, 5. 40 Academy Hill Rd, Brighton ☎ 782-6032

Charlestown, 30. 179 Main St, Charlestown ☎ 242-1248

Codman Sq, 27. 690 Washington St, Dorchester ☎ 436-8214

Connolly, 14. 433 Centre St, Jamaica Plain ☎ 522-1960

Dudley, 11. 65 Warren St, Roxbury ☎ 442-6186

East Boston, 2. 276 Meridian St, E Boston ☎ 569-0271

Egleston Sq, 15. 2044 Columbus Ave, Roxbury ☎ 445-4340

Faneuil, 4. 419 Faneuil St, Brighton ☎ 782-6705

Fields Corner, 22. 1520 Dorchester Ave, Dorchester ☎ 436-2155

Grove Hall, 18. 5 Crawford St, Dorchester ☎ 427-3337

Hyde Park, 26. 35 Harvard St, Hyde Park ☎ 361-2524

Jamaica Plain, 17. 12 Sedgwick St, Jamaica Plain ☎ 524-2053

Kirstein Business, 37. 20 City Hall Ave ☎ 523-0860

Lower Mills, 28. 27 Richmond St, Dorchester ☎ 298-7841

Mattapan, 25. 8 Hazleton St, Mattapan ☎ 298-9218

North End, 31. 25 Parmenter St ☎ 227-8135

Orient Heights, 3. 18 Barnes Ave, E Boston ☎ 567-2516

Parker Hill, 10. 1497 Tremont St, Roxbury ☎ 427-3820

Roslindale, 24. 4238 Washington St, Roslindale ☎ 323-2343

South Boston, 13. 646 E Broadway, S Boston ☎ 268-0180

Uphams Corner, 19. 500 Columbia Rd, Dorchester ☎ 265-0139

Washington Village, 12. 1226 Columbia Rd, S Boston ☎ 269-7239

West End, 32. 151 Cambridge St ☎ 523-3957

West Roxbury, 23. 1961 Centre St, W Roxbury ☎ 325-3147

PROFESSIONAL

Archives of American Art, 33. 87 Mt Vernon St ☎ 565-4444

Arnold Arboretum, 16. Arborway, Jamaica Plain ☎ 524-1718

Art Institute Boston, 7. 700 Beacon St ☎ 262-1223

Boston Architecture, 47. 320 Newbury St ☎ 536-9018

Boston Athenaeum, 36. 10 1/2 Beacon St ☎ 227-0270

Boston Globe Newspaper, 20. 135 Morrissey Blvd ☎ 929-2540

Boston Herald Newspaper, 52. 300 Harrison Ave ☎ 426-3000

Boston Psychoanalytic, 41. 15 Commonwealth Ave ☎ 266-0953

Bostonian Society, 38. 15 State St ☎ 720-3285

Charles River Association, 45. 200 Clarendon St ☎ 266-0500

Christian Science Monitor, 49. 1 Norway St ☎ 450-2000

Congregational Library, 35. 14 Beacon St ☎ 523-0470

Crime & Justice Foundation, 42. 20 West St ☎ 426-9800

Federal Reserve Bank, 43. 600 Atlantic Ave ☎ 973-3397

Franklin Institute, 51. 41 Berkeley St ☎ 423-4630

French Library, 40. 53 Marlborough St ☎ 266-4351

General Theological, 34. 14 Beacon St ☎ 227-4557

Goethe Institute, 39. 170 Beacon St ☎ 262-6050

Kennedy National, 21. Columbia Pt, Dorchester ☎ 929-4500

Mass Historical Society, 48. 1154 Boylston St ☎ 536-1608

Mass Horticultural Society, 50. 300 Mass Ave ☎ 536-9280

Museum of Fine Arts, 9. 465 Huntington Ave ☎ 267-9300

New Eng Genealogical Society, 44. 101 Newbury St ☎ 536-5740

Smithsonian Astrophysical, 1. 60 Garden St, Cambridge ☎ 495-7461

Temple Israel, 8. 260 Riverway ☎ 566-3960

Zion Research, 6. 771 Commonwealth Ave ☎ 353-3724

MAP 12 Universities, Colleges & Schools

Listed by Site Number

1 Radcliffe College	**13** Fisher College	**24** Simmons College
2 Harvard Law	**14** Emerson College	**25** New England
3 Lesley College	**15** Bay State College	Conservatory of
4 Harvard University	**16** New Eng College of	Music
5 Harvard Business	Optometry	**26** Northeastern Univ
6 Bunker Hill CC	**17** Newbury College	**27** Boston Univ Dental
7 Mass Inst Tech (MIT)	**18** Berklee Col of Music	**28** Boston Univ Medical
8 Suffolk University	**19** Boston Conservatory	**29** Wentworth Inst Tech
9 Suffolk Law	of Music	**30** Mass College of Art
10 Tufts Dental	**20** Boston University	**31** Mass Col Pharmacy
11 Tufts Medical	**21** Hebrew College	**32** Harvard Medical
12 New Eng Sch of Law	**22** Wheelock College	**33** Roxbury CC
	23 Emmanuel College	**34** Hellenic College

MAP 12

Listed Alphabetically

Bay State College, 15.
122 Commonwealth Ave
☎ 236-8000

Berklee College of Music, 18.
1140 Boylston St
☎ 266-1400

Boston Conservatory of Music, 19.
8 Fenway
☎ 536-6340

Boston University, 20.
770 Commonwealth Ave
☎ 353-2000

**Boston University Medical Center–
Goldman Graduate School of
Dentistry, 27.** 100 E Newton St
☎ 638-4700

**Boston University Medical Center
Campus, 28.**
88 E Newton St
☎ 638-8000

Bunker Hill Community College, 6.
Rutherford Ave, Charlestown
☎ 241-8600

Emerson College, 14. 100 Beacon St
☎ 578-8500

Emmanuel College, 23.
400 Fenway
☎ 277-9340

Fisher College, 13.
118 Beacon St
☎ 236-8800

Harvard University, 4.
33 Kirkland St, Cambridge
☎ 495-1000

Harvard Business School, 5.
16 No Harvard St, Allston
☎ 495-6000

Harvard Law School, 2.
Massachusetts Ave, Cambridge
☎ 495-3100

Harvard Medical, 32.
25 Shattuck St
☎ 432-1000

Hebrew College, 21.
43 Hawes St, Brookline
☎ 232-8710

Hellenic College, 34.
50 Goddard Ave, Brookline
☎ 731-3500

Lesley College, 3.
29 Everett St, Cambridge
☎ 868-9600

Massachusetts College of Art, 30.
621 Huntington Ave
☎ 232-1555

**Massachusetts College of
Pharmacy and Allied Health
Sciences, 31.**
179 Longwood Ave
☎ 732-2800

**Massachusetts Institute of
Technology (MIT), 7.**
77 Massachusetts Ave, Cambridge
☎ 253-1000

**New England College of
Optometry, 16.**
424 Beacon St
☎ 266-2030

**New England Conservatory of
Music, 25.**
290 Huntington Ave
☎ 262-1120

New England School of Law, 12.
154 Stuart St
☎ 451-0010

Newbury College, 17.
921 Boylston St
☎ 730-7044

Northeastern University, 26.
360 Huntington Ave
☎ 437-2000

Radcliffe College, 1.
10 Garden St, Cambridge
☎ 495-8000

Roxbury Community College, 33.
1234 Columbus Ave, Roxbury
☎ 427-0060

Simmons College, 24.
300 Fenway
☎ 738-2000

Suffolk University, 8.
8 Ashburton Pl
☎ 723-4700

Suffolk University Law School, 9.
41 Temple St
☎ 573-8000

**Tufts University School of Dental
Medicine, 10.**
1 Kneeland St
☎ 956-6639

**Tufts University School of
Medicine, 11.** 136 Harrison Ave
☎ 956-7000

**Wentworth Institute of
Technology, 29.**
550 Huntington Ave
☎ 442-9010

Wheelock College, 22.
200 Riverway
☎ 734-5200

MAP **13** **Universities & Colleges/Boston Area**

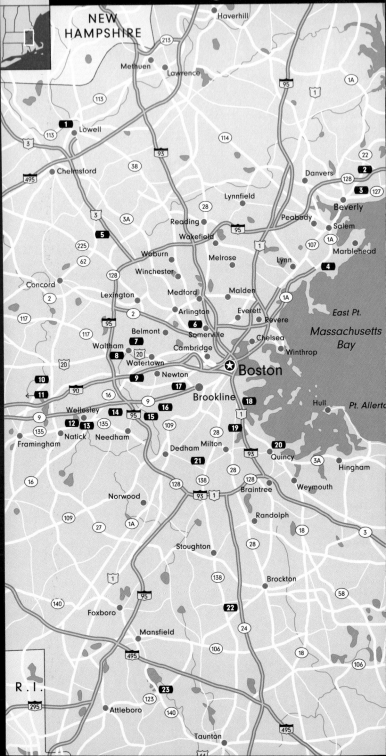

MAP 13

Listed by Site Number

1 University of Massachusetts–Lowell
2 Gordon College
3 Endicott College
4 Salem State College
5 Middlesex Community College
6 Tufts University
7 Bentley College
8 Brandeis University
9 Lasell College
10 Regis College
11 Tufts University School of Veterinary Medicine
12 Wellesley College
13 Babson College
14 Massachusetts Bay Community College
15 Mount Ida College
16 Pine Manor College
17 Boston College
18 University of Massachusetts–Boston
19 Laboure Junior College
20 Eastern Nazarene College
21 Curry College
22 Stonehill College
23 Wheaton College

Listed Alphabetically

Babson College, 13.
Wellesley Ave, Wellesley
☎ 235-1200

Bentley College, 7.
Forest St, Waltham
☎ 891-2000

Boston College, 17.
140 Commonwealth Ave, Chestnut Hill
☎ 552-8000

Brandeis University, 8.
415 South St, Waltham
☎ 736-2000

Curry College, 21.
1071 Blue Hill Ave, Milton
☎ 333-0500

Eastern Nazarene College, 20.
23 E Elm St, Wollaston ☎ 773-6350

Endicott College, 3.
376 Hale St, Beverly
☎ 508/921-1000

Gordon College, 2.
255 Grapevine Rd, Wenham
☎ 508/927-2300

Laboure Junior College, 19.
2120 Dorchester Ave
☎ 296-8300

Lasell College, 9.
1844 Commonwealth Ave, Newton
☎ 243-2000

Massachusetts Bay Community College, 14.
50 Oakland St, Wellesley
☎ 237-1100

Middlesex Comunity College, 5.
Springs Rd, Bedford
☎ 275-8910

Mount Ida College, 15.
777 Dedham St, Newton
☎ 969-7000

Pine Manor College, 16.
400 Heath St, Chestnut Hill
☎ 731-7000

Regis College, 10.
235 Wellesley St, Weston
☎ 893-1820

Salem State College, 4.
352 Lafayette St, Salem
☎ 508/741-6000

Stonehill College, 22.
320 Washington Ave, Easton
☎ 508/238-1081

Tufts University, 6.
Packard Ave, Medford
☎ 628-5000

Tufts University School of Veterinary Medicine, 11.
Westboro Rd, North Grafton
☎ 508/839-5302

University of Massachusetts–Boston, 18.
Columbia Bay, Dorchester
☎ 287-5000

University of Massachusetts–Lowell, 1.
1 University Ave, Lowell
☎ 508/934-4000

Wellesley College, 12.
106 Central St, Wellesley
☎ 283-1000

Wheaton College, 23.
E Main St, Norton
☎ 508/285-7722

MAP 14 Harvard and Radcliffe

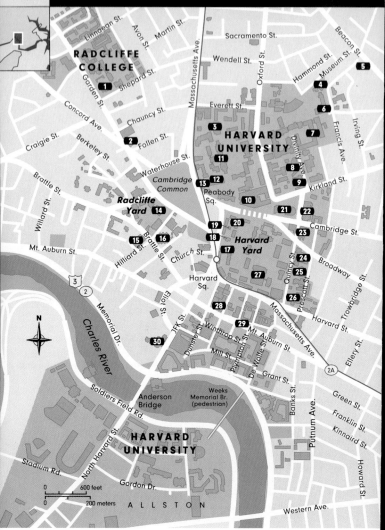

Listed by Site Number

Massachusetts Institute of Technology

MAP 15

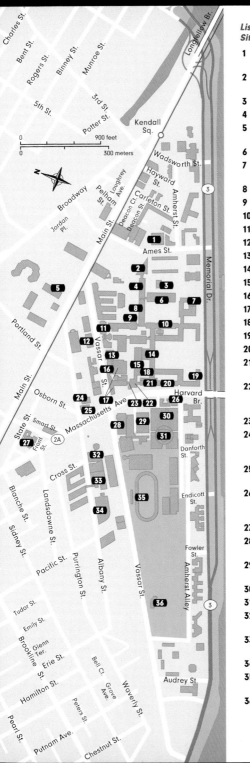

Listed by Site Number

1   List Visual Arts Centre
2   Ralph Landau Building
3   Green Building
4   Whitaker Building
5   Laboratory for Computer Science
6   Dreyfus Building
7   Hayden Memorial Library
8   Dorrance Building
9   Compton Labs
10   Eastman Labs
11   Fairchild Building
12   Cyclotron
13   Brown Building
14   Maclaurin Bldgs
15   Bush Building
16   McNair Building
17   Sloan Laboratories
18   Homberg Building
19   Pierce Laboratory
20   Pratt School
21   Rogers Bldg/Hart Nautical Gallery
22   Center for Advanced Engineering Study
23   Guggenheim Lab
24   Superconducting Generator Test Facility
25   High Voltage Research Lab
26   Center for Advanced Visual Studies
27   MIT Museum
28   du Pont Athletic Center
29   Stratton Building Student Center
30   MIT Chapel
31   Kresge Auditorium
32   Nuclear Reactor Laboratory
33   F Bitter National Magnet Laboratory
34   Nabisco Lab
35   Steinbrenner Stadium
36   MIT Solar Demo Building

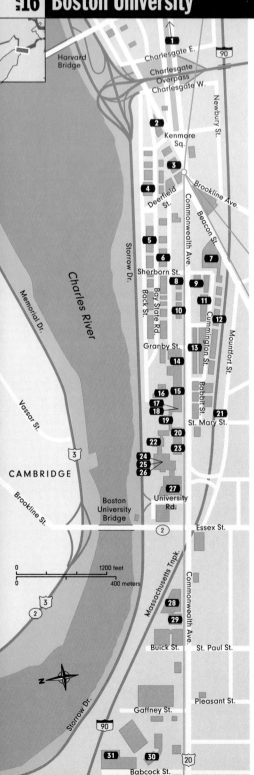

MAP 16 **Boston University**

Harvard Bridge

Charlesgate E.
Charlesgate Overpass
Charlesgate W.

Newbury St.

90

Kenmore Sq.

Brookline Ave.

Deerfield St.

Commonwealth Ave.

Beacon St.

Storrow Dr.

Sherborn St.

Back St.

Bay State Rd.

Charles River

Memorial Dr.

Cummington St.

Mountfort St.

Granby St.

Babbitt St.

St. Mary St.

Vassar St.

3

CAMBRIDGE

Brookline St.

Boston University Bridge

University Rd.

2

Essex St.

0   1200 feet
0   400 meters

3
2

Commonwealth Ave.

Massachusetts Tpke.

Buick St.   St. Paul St.

N

Starrow Dr.

90

Gaffney St.   Pleasant St.

31   30   20

Babcock St.

Logan International Airport MAP 17

Airline	Terminal	A	B	C	D	E
Aer Lingus ☎ 800/223-6537						●
Air Alliance ☎ 800/776-3000						●
Air Atlantic/Canadian Air ☎ 800/426-7000						●
Air Canada ☎ 800/776-3000						●
Air France ☎ 800/237-2747						●
Air Nova ☎ 800/776-3000						●
Alitalia ☎ 800/223-5730	(Departures Only)				●	
	(Int'l Arrivals Only)					●
American ☎ 800/433-7300			●			
	(Int'l Arrivals Only)					●
American Eagle ☎ 800/433-7300			●			
American Trans Air ☎ 800/543-3710				●		
American West ☎ 800/247-5692			●			
Atlantic North ☎ 800/553-9021						●
British Airways ☎ 800/247-9297						●
Business Express/Delta Connection ☎ 800/345-3400				●		
Cape Air ☎ 800/352-0714		●				
Colgan Air ☎ 800/272-5488		●				
Continental ☎ 800/525-0280		●				
Delta Airlines ☎ 800/221-1212		●				
Delta Shuttle ☎ 800/221-1212	(LaGuardia only)		●			
El Al Israel Airlines ☎ 800/223-6700						●
KLM ☎ 800/374-7747						●
Lufthansa ☎ 800/645-3880						●
Midwest Express ☎ 800/452-2022			●			
Northeast Express/NW Airlink ☎ 800/225-2525						●
Northwest ☎ 800/225-2525						●
Olympic ☎ 800/223-1226						●
Qantas ☎ 800/227-4500			●			
Spirit Airlines ☎ 800/772-7117		●				
Swissair ☎ 800/221-4750						●
TAP Air Portugal ☎ 800/221-7370						●
TWA ☎ 800/221-2000				●		
	(Int'l Arrivals Only)					●
TW Express ☎ 800/221-2000				●		
United/United Express ☎ 800/241-6522				●		
US Air/US Air Express ☎ 800/428-4322			●			
US Air Shuttle ☎ 800/428-4322	(LaGuardia only)	●				
Virgin Atlantic ☎ 800/862-8621	(Int'l Arrivals Only)					●
	(Departures Only)		●			

MAP **18** **Driving & Parking/Downtown**

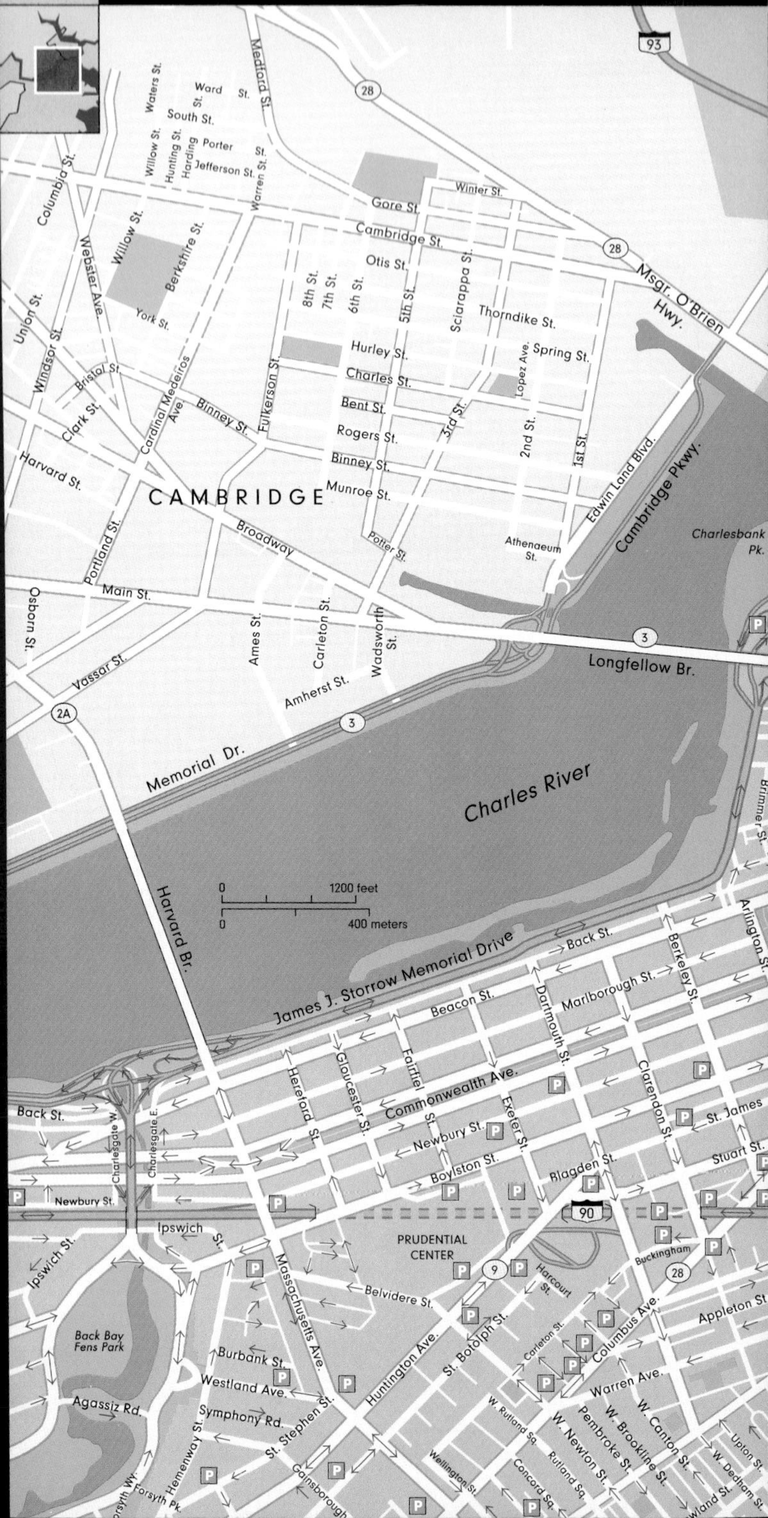

93

Waters St.
Ward St.
South St.
Medford St.
Willow St.
Harding
Porter
Hunting St.
Jefferson St.
28
Winter St.
Columbia St.
Warren St.
Gore St.
Cambridge St.
28
Otis St.
Webster Ave.
Berkshire St.
York St.
8th St.
7th St.
6th St.
5th St.
4th St.
Sciarappa St.
Thorndike St.
Msgr. O'Brien Hwy.
Union St.
Windsor St.
Bristol St.
Clark St.
Cardinal Medeiros Ave.
Fulkerson St.
Hurley St.
Charles St.
Spring St.
Lopez Ave.
Harvard St.
Binney St.
Bent St.
Rogers St.
3rd St.
2nd St.
1st St.
Edwin Land Blvd.
Charlesbank Pk.

Binney St.
C A M B R I D G E
Munroe St.
Potter St.
Athenaeum St.
Cambridge Pkwy.

Portland St.
Broadway
Osborn St.
Main St.
Ames St.
Carleton St.
Wadsworth St.

3
Longfellow Br.

Vassar St.
Amherst St.

2A
3

Memorial Dr.

Charles River

Harvard Br.

0   1200 feet
0   400 meters

James J. Storrow Memorial Drive
Back St.
Beacon St.
Marlborough St.
Berkeley St.
Arlington St.
Fairfield St.
Dartmouth St.
Back St.
Hereford St.
Gloucester St.
Commonwealth Ave.
Exeter St.
Clarendon St.
St. James
Charlesgate W.
Charlesgate E.
Newbury St.
Blagden St.
Stuart St.
Newbury St.
Boylston St.
90
Ipswich
Buckingham
Ipswich St.
Massachusetts Ave.
PRUDENTIAL CENTER
9
Harcourt St.
28
Belvidere St.
Columbus Ave.
Appleton St.
Back Bay Fens Park
Burbank St.
Huntington Ave.
St. Botolph St.
Corerton St.
Warren St.
W. Canton St.
Westland Ave.
W. Brookline St.
W. Newton St.
Agassiz Rd.
Symphony Rd.
St. Stephen St.
Pembroke St.
W. Rutland Sq.
W. Dedham St.
Hemenway St.
Forsyth Pk.
Gainsborough St.
Wellington St.
Concord Sq.
E. Rutland Sq.

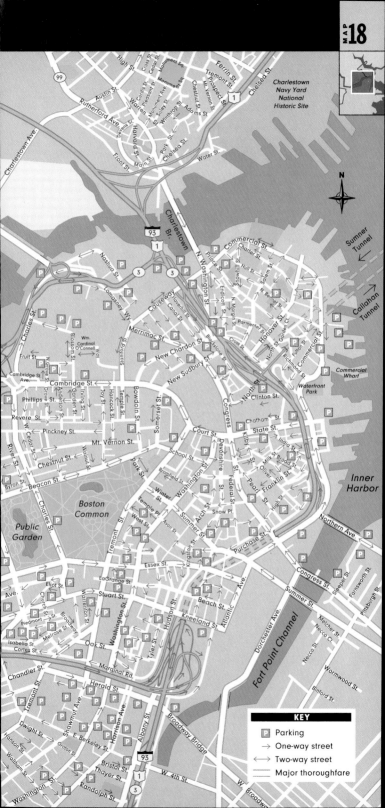

MAP **19** **MBTA Rapid Transit/Downtown**

SOMERVILLE

Linwood St.
Joy St.
Fitchburg St.

Tremont St.
Ward St.
South St.
Medford St.
Winter St.

Cambridge St.
Willow St.
Harding St.
Porter
Warren St.
Jefferson St.

Norfolk St.
Elm St.
Columbia St.
Cambridge St.
Gore St.

Hampshire St.
Union St.
Windsor Ave.
Willow St.
Cambridge St.

28

LECHMERE

Msgr.

Windsor St.
Donnelly Field
Otis St.
Sciarappa St.
Thorndike St.
Spring St.

Market St.
Berkshire St.
8th St.
7th St.
6th St.
5th St.
John Ahearn Field
Hurley St.
Charles St.
Lopez Ave.
2nd St.

Cherry St.
Bristol St.
Clark St.
Cardinal Medeiros Ave.
Binney St.
Bent
3rd St.
1st St.

Harvard St.
Washington St.
CAMBRIDGE
Rogers St.
Binney St.
Munroe St.
Athenaeum St.

Allen Dr.
Portland St.
Broadway
Potter St.
Edwin Land Blvd.
Cambridge Pkwy.

State St.
Main St.
KENDALL
Longfellow Br.

Massachusetts Ave.
Osborn St.
Ames St.
Carleton St.
Amherst St.

Lansdowne St.
Cross St.
Albany St.
Vassar St.
2A

3

Briggs Field (MIT)
Memorial Dr.
Amherst St.
Danforth St.
Charles River

Amherst Al.
Fowler St.
Endicott St.
Harvard Br.

0 — 1200 feet
0 — 400 meters

James J. Storrow Memorial Drive
Back St.
Berkeley St.

Bay State Rd.
Back St.
Deerfield St.
Raleigh St.
Charlesgate W.
Charlesgate E.
Beacon St.
Marlborough St.
Clarendon St.
BACK BAY

20
Kenmore Sq.
Fairfield St.
Dartmouth St.
Exeter St.

Beacon St.
Newbury St.
Commonwealth Ave.
COPLEY

90
KENMORE
Newbury St.
Boylston St.
Gloucester St.
Hereford St.
Blagden St.
BACK BAY/ SOUTH END

Lansdowne St.
Ipswich St.
ICA/CONV CTR (Auditorium)
PRUDENTIAL CENTER
90
28

Brookline Ave.
Yawkey Way
Fenway Park
Belvidere St.
Harcourt St.
Chandler

Van Ness St.
THE FENS
Back Bay Fens Park
Norway St.
Burbank St.
PRUDENTIAL
9
Columbus Ave.
Warren
W. Newton St.
W. Canton St.

Boylston St.
Jersey St.
Peterborough St.
Westland Ave.
Symphony Rd.
St. Stephen St.
Massachusetts Ave.
St. Botolph St.
Huntington Ave.
Carleton St.
Penbroke St.
W. Newton St.
Tremont St.

Kilmarnock St.
Queensberry St.
Park Dr.
SYMPHONY
W. Rutland Sq.
Rutland St.
Concord St.
Worcester St.
Rutland St.

Forsyth Way
Forsyth Pk.
Gainsborough St.
MASSACHUSETTS AVE
Massachusetts Ave.
Northampton St.
W. Springfield St.
Blackstone Sq.

Forsyth St.
NORTHEASTERN
Columbus Ave.
Newland St.

Pond Rd.
MUSEUM
Huntington Ave.
RUGGLES

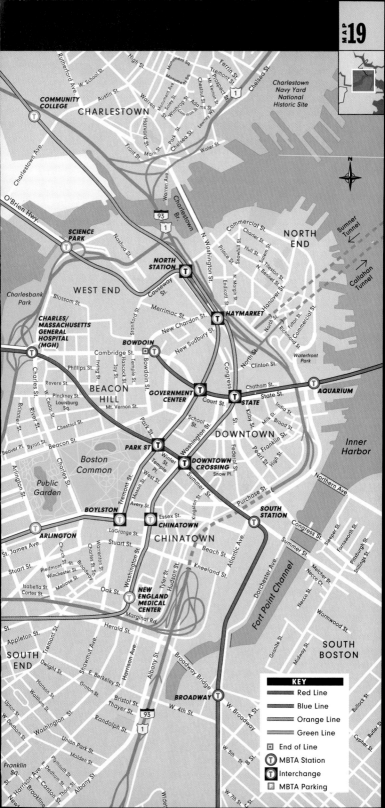

MAP 20 MBTA Rapid Transit/Boston Area

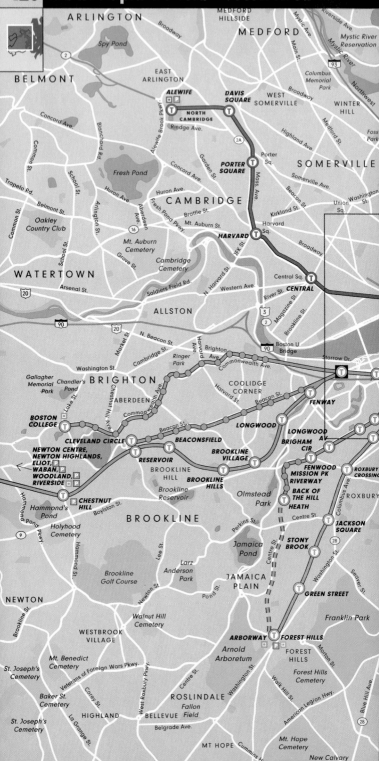

ARLINGTON

MEDFORD
HILLSIDE

MEDFORD

Mystic River
Reservation

Spy Pond

Broadway

Columbus
Memorial
Park

BELMONT

EAST
ARLINGTON

WEST
SOMERVILLE

WINTER
HILL

Foss
Park

ALEWIFE

DAVIS
SQUARE

NORTH
CAMBRIDGE

Rindge Ave.

SOMERVILLE

Concord Ave.

Fresh Pond

PORTER
SQUARE

Porter
Sq.

Somerville Ave.

Union
Sq.

Washington
St.

Oakley
Country Club

CAMBRIDGE

Mt. Auburn
Cemetery

Cambridge
Cemetery

Harvard
Sq.

HARVARD

Broadway

WATERTOWN

Arsenal St.

Soldiers Field Rd.

Western Ave.

CENTRAL

Central Sq.

ALLSTON

Boston U.
Bridge

Storrow Dr.

BRIGHTON

Ringer
Park

Commonwealth Ave.

COOLIDGE
CORNER

FENWAY

Gallagher
Memorial
Park

Chandler's
Pond

Washington St.

LONGWOOD

LONGWOOD
AV

BOSTON
COLLEGE

ABERDEEN

Beacon St.

BRIGHAM
CIR

ROXBURY
CROSSING

CLEVELAND CIRCLE

RESERVOIR

BEACONSFIELD

BROOKLINE
VILLAGE

FENWOOD
MISSION PK
RIVERWAY

NEWTON CENTRE,
NEWTON HIGHLANDS,
ELIOT,
WABAN,
WOODLAND,
RIVERSIDE

Brookline
Hill

BROOKLINE
HILLS

BACK OF
THE HILL
HEATH

ROXBURY

CHESTNUT
HILL

Hammond's
Pond

Brookline
Reservoir

Olmstead
Park

JACKSON
SQUARE

Holyhood
Cemetery

BROOKLINE

Jamaica
Pond

STONY
BROOK

NEWTON

Brookline
Golf Course

Larz
Anderson
Park

JAMAICA
PLAIN

GREEN STREET

Franklin
Park

WESTBROOK
VILLAGE

Walnut Hill
Cemetery

St. Joseph's
Cemetery

Mt. Benedict
Cemetery

ARBORWAY

FOREST HILLS

Arnold
Arboretum

FOREST
HILLS

Baker St.
Cemetery

HIGHLAND

ROSLINDALE

Fallon
Field

Forest Hills
Cemetery

St. Joseph's
Cemetery

BELLEVUE

Belgrade Ave.

MT HOPE

Mt. Hope
Cemetery

New Calvary

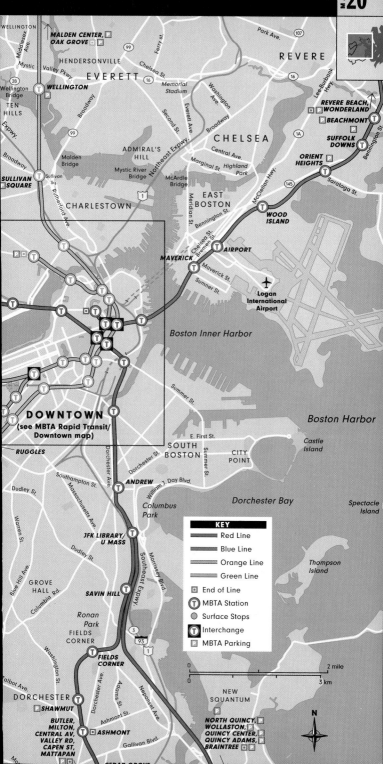

MAP **20**

WELLINGTON

MALDEN CENTER, OAK GROVE

HENDERSONVILLE

Park Ave. 107

REVERE

Mystic

Middlesex Ave.

EVERETT

Ferry st.

Chelsea St.

Memorial Stadium

16

Lee-Burbank Hwy.

16

REVERE BEACH, WONDERLAND

BEACHMONT

Valley Pkwy.

WELLINGTON

Broadway

Second St.

Washington Ave.

Everett Ave.

Broadway

1A

SUFFOLK DOWNS

Bennington St.

28

Wellington Bridge

TEN HILLS

Expwy.

99

Sullivan Sq.

CHELSEA

Central Ave.

Highland Park

ORIENT HEIGHTS

Saratoga St.

Broadway

ADMIRAL'S HILL

Malden Bridge

Mystic River Bridge

Northeast Expwy.

McArdle Bridge

Marginal St.

McClellan Hwy.

145

WOOD ISLAND

SULLIVAN SQUARE

Sullivan Sq.

Rutherford Ave.

CHARLESTOWN

1

Meridian St.

EAST BOSTON

Chelsea St.

Bremen St.

Bennington St.

MAVERICK

AIRPORT

Maverick St.

Sumner St.

Logan International Airport

Boston Inner Harbor

DOWNTOWN
(see MBTA Rapid Transit/ Downtown map)

RUGGLES

Dorchester Ave.

Southampton St.

Massachusetts Ave.

Dudley St.

Warren St.

SOUTH BOSTON

E. First St.

Summer St.

CITY POINT

Boston Harbor

Castle Island

ANDREW

Dorchester St.

William J. Day Blvd.

Columbus Park

Dorchester Bay

Spectacle Island

JFK LIBRARY/ U MASS

Dudley St.

Southeast Expwy.

Morrissey Blvd.

Thompson Island

GROVE HALL

Blue Hill Ave.

Columbia Rd.

SAVIN HILL

Ronan Park

FIELDS CORNER

3

93

1

KEY	
	Red Line
	Blue Line
	Orange Line
	Green Line
▫	End of Line
Ⓣ	MBTA Station
●	Surface Stops
Ⓣ	Interchange
▫	MBTA Parking

FIELDS CORNER

Washington St.

Talbot Ave.

Dorchester Ave.

Adams St.

Neponset Ave.

DORCHESTER

SHAWMUT

BUTLER, MILTON, CENTRAL AV, VALLEY RD, CAPEN ST, MATTAPAN

ASHMONT

Ashmont St.

Gallivan Blvd.

NEW SQUANTUM

NORTH QUINCY, WOLLASTON, QUINCY CENTER, QUINCY ADAMS, BRAINTREE

0 ──────── 2 mile
0 ──────── 3 km

N

CEDAR GROVE

MAP 21 Buses/Downtown

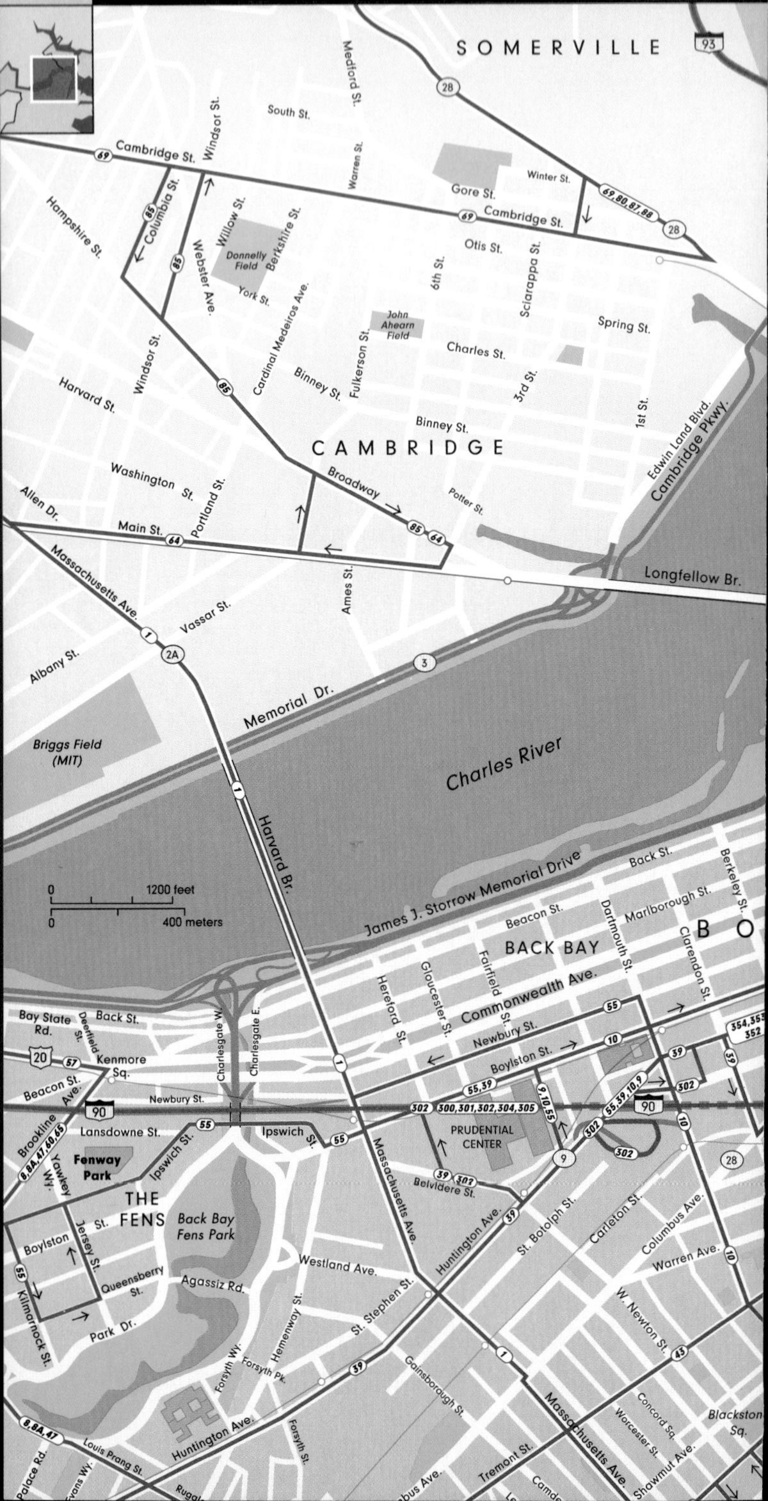

SOMERVILLE

95

CAMBRIDGE

Cambridge St.
Windsor St.
South St.
Medford St.
Warren St.
Winter St.
Gore St.
Cambridge St.
Otis St.
Sciarappa St.
Spring St.
6th St.
Hampshire St.
Columbia St.
Willow St.
Berkshire St.
York St.
Donnelly Field
Cardinal Medeiros Ave.
Binney St.
Fulkerson St.
John Ahearn Field
Charles St.
3rd St.
1st St.
Edwin Land Blvd.
Cambridge Pkwy.
Binney St.
Harvard St.
Webster Ave.
Washington St.
Portland St.
Broadway
Potter St.
Allen Dr.
Main St.
Ames St.
Massachusetts Ave.
Albany St.
Vassar St.
Windsor St.
Longfellow Br.

Memorial Dr.

Harvard Br.

Briggs Field (MIT)

Charles River

James J. Storrow Memorial Drive

Beacon St.
Back St.
Berkeley St.
Marlborough St.
Dartmouth St.
Clarendon St.

BACK BAY

BO

Commonwealth Ave.

Hereford St.
Gloucester St.
Fairfield St.

Newbury St.

Boylston St.

354,355
352

Bay State Rd.
Back St.
Deerfield St.
Charlesgate W.
Charlesgate E.

Kenmore Sq.
Newbury St.
Ipswich St.
Ipswich St.

Beacon St.
Brookline Ave.
Lansdowne St.
Fenway Park
Yawkey Way
Jersey St.

55

502 300,301,302,304,305

PRUDENTIAL CENTER

Belvidere St.

Massachusetts Ave.

THE FENS

Back Bay Fens Park

Boylston St.
Queensberry St.
Agassiz Rd.
Westland Ave.
St. Stephen St.
Huntington Ave.
St. Botolph St.
Carleton St.
Columbus Ave.
Warren St.
Park Dr.
W. Newton St.

Kilmarnock St.
Forsyth Way
Hemenway St.
Forsyth Pk.
Gainsborough St.
Concord Sq.
Blackston
Huntington Ave.
Forsyth St.

Palace Rd.
Louis Prang St.
Evans Way
Ruggles St.
Columbus Ave.
Tremont St.
Worcester St.
Shawmut Ave.

1200 feet
400 meters

69
85
64
3
1
2A
85 64
20
57
90
8A,47,48,55
8,8A,47
55
9
39
502
10
352
10,9,55
55,59
39
503
43
28
69, 80, 87, 88

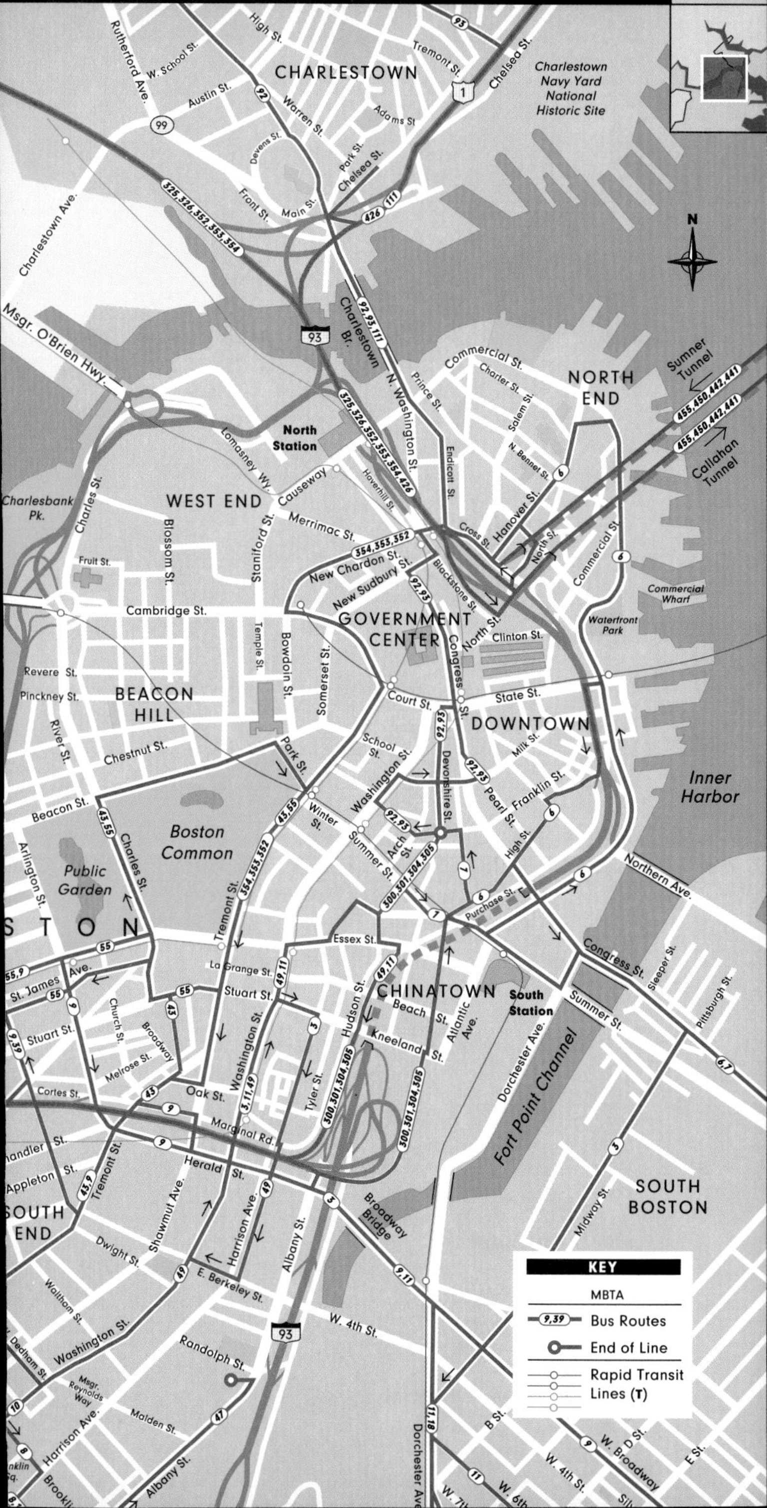
CHARLESTOWN
Charlestown Navy Yard National Historic Site
NORTH END
North Station
WEST END
GOVERNMENT CENTER
BEACON HILL
DOWNTOWN
Boston Common
Public Garden
CHINATOWN
South Station
Fort Point Channel
SOUTH BOSTON
SOUTH END
Inner Harbor
Charlesbank Pk.
Commercial Wharf
Waterfront Park
Sumner Tunnel
Callahan Tunnel
Charlestown Br.
Broadway Bridge
High St.
Tremont St.
Chelsea St.
Rutherford Ave.
W. School St.
Austin St.
Warren St.
Adams St
Devens St.
Park St.
Front St.
Main St.
Charlestown Ave.
Msgr. O'Brien Hwy.
Lomasney Wy.
Causeway
Haverhill St.
N. Washington St.
Commercial St.
Charter St.
Prince St.
Salem St.
N. Bennet St.
Endicott St.
Hanover St.
Cross St.
North St.
Charles St.
Fruit St.
Blossom St.
Staniford St.
Merrimac St.
New Chardon St.
New Sudbury St.
Blackstone St.
Clinton St.
Cambridge St.
Temple St.
Bowdoin St.
Somerset St.
Congress St.
Revere St.
Pinckney St.
River St.
Court St.
State St.
Chestnut St.
School St.
Milk St.
Park St.
Washington St.
Devonshire St.
Franklin St.
Pearl St.
Beacon St.
Winter St.
Summer St.
Arch St.
High St.
Northern Ave.
Arlington St.
Purchase St.
Essex St.
Congress St.
Sleeper St.
Pittsburgh St.
La Grange St.
St. James Ave.
Stuart St.
Hudson St.
Beach St.
Atlantic Ave.
Summer St.
Church St.
Broadway
Melrose St.
Kneeland St.
Dorchester Ave.
Tyler St.
Cortes St.
Oak St.
Marginal Rd.
Chandler St.
Appleton St.
Herald St.
Shawmut Ave.
Harrison Ave.
Albany St.
Midway St.
Dwight St.
E. Berkeley St.
Waltham St.
Washington St.
W. 4th St.
Randolph St.
Dedham St.
Msgr. Reynolds Way
Malden St.
Harrison Ave.
Albany St.
Franklin Sq.
Brookline
B St.
W. 4th St.
W. 6th
W. Broadway
D St.
E St.
Dorchester Ave.
325,326,352,353,354
92,93,111
325,326,352,353,354,426
354,353,352
92,93
455,450,442,441
43,55
354,353,352
300,301,304,305
49,11
3,11,49
300,301,504,305
92,93
KEY
MBTA
9,39 Bus Routes
End of Line
Rapid Transit Lines (T)
N

MAP 22 Buses/Boston Area

ARLINGTON

Concord Tnpk.

Spy Pond

Broadway

Clarendon Hill

Tufts University

Powder House Square

BELMONT

North Cambridge

Massachusetts Ave.

Belmont Center

Concord Ave.

Russell Field

Rindge Ave.

Porter Sq.

Waverley

Trapelo Rd.

Belmont St.

Fresh Pond

Concord Ave.

Huron Ave.

Ridgelawn Cemetery

Oakley Country Club

Huron Ave.

Massachusetts Ave.

Harvard Sq.

Aberdeen Avenue

Mt. Auburn St.

Harvard University

WATERTOWN

Main St.

Mt. Auburn St.

16

Mt. Auburn Cemetery

JFK St.

N. Harvard St.

BEMIS

Allison Park

Watertown St.

16

Watertown Square

Watertown Yard

Arsenal St.

Western Ave.

ALLSTON

N. Beacon St.

Union Sq.

Brighton Ave.

Market St.

Cambridge St.

Ringer Park

Harvard Ave.

Commonwealth Ave.

Magazine

Newton Corner

Massachusetts Tnpk.

Cabot Park

Centre St.

Oak Square

Brighton Center

Washington St.

Chandler Pond

BRIGHTON

Chestnut Hill Ave.

Commonwealth Ave.

Harvard St.

Beacon

Coolidge Corner

Edwards Park

NEWTON

Boston College

Chestnut Hill Res.

Cleveland Circle

Beacon St.

Hammond's Pond

Boylston St.

Brookline Reservoir

Olmstead Park

Oak Hill Playground

Hammond Pond Park Reservation

Chestnut Hill

Holyhood Cemetery

BROOKLINE

Lee St.

Jamaica Pond

JAMAICA PLAIN

Parker St.

Brookline Golf Course

Larz Anderson Park

Monument

Centre St.

Oak Hill

Dedham Rd.

Nahanton St.

Walnut Hill Cemetery

Arnold Arboretum

Washington St.

Mt. Benedict Cemetery

St. Joseph's Cemetery

Baker St. Cemetery

Mt. Lebanon

Corey St.

Centre St.

ROSLINDALE

KEY

MBTA

9,59   Bus Routes

End of Line

Rapid Transit Lines (T)

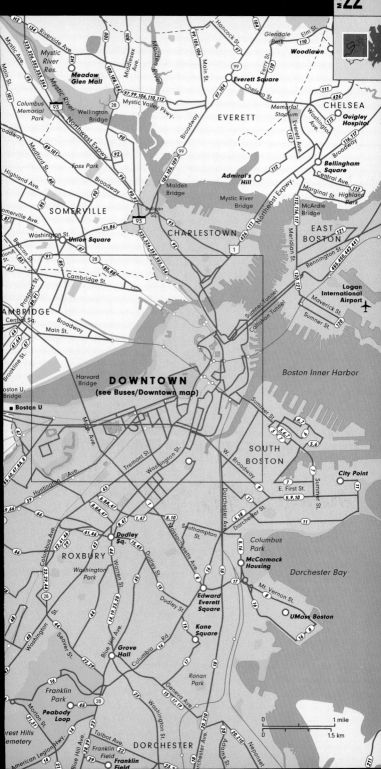

MAP 22

H2

134 Riverside Ave.

100

801

Middlesex Ave.

Main St.

99,105,106

Hancock St.

184

Glendale Park

Elm St.

110

Woodlawn

H2

H2

Mystic Ave.

Mystic River Res.

Meadow Glen Mall

134, 352, 353, 355, 356

100, 108, 110

97, 99, 106, 110, 112

Mystic Valley Pkwy.

99

Everett Square

97, 104

Ferry St.

Chelsea St.

111

426

CHELSEA

Quigley Hospital

Columbus Memorial Park

93

Northwest Expwy.

Wellington Bridge

90

Memorial Stadium

112

Washington Ave.

116, 117

Broadway

Main St.

95

101

Medford St.

95, 101

Foss Park

89

Broadway

95

Highland Ave.

90, 92

92

99

104, 105, 106

Malden Bridge

Admiral's Hill

Mystic River Bridge

Everett Ave.

112

Northeast Expwy.

112

Bellingham Square

Central Ave.

Marginal St.

112

Highland Park

McArdle Bridge

EVERETT

EAST BOSTON

121

somerville Ave.

SOMERVILLE

89

91, 86

93

Sullivan Sq.

93

1

475, 111

Meridian St.

120, 121

455, 459, 442, 441

Bennington St.

Washington St.

Union Square

87

28

80, 88

CHARLESTOWN

92

Logan International Airport

land St.

83

69

91

86

Cambridge St.

Sumner Tunnel

Callahan Tunnel

Maverick St.

Sumner St.

120

CAMBRIDGE

Central Sq.

64

Broadway

Main St.

47, 44

87

Sumner St.

170

Brookline Ave.

ston U. Bridge

Harvard Bridge

DOWNTOWN
(see Buses/Downtown map)

Boston Inner Harbor

Boston U

CT1

Mass. Ave.

Tremont St.

Washington St.

W. Broadway

SOUTH BOSTON

Sumner St.

6, 7

5, 6, 7

6

5, 6

7

9, 66

66

Huntington Ave.

43

9, 40, 47, 8, 8

E. First St.

City Point

111

9

8, 8A, 47

5, 9, 10

Sumner St.

7

1

8, 8A, 47

Dorchester Ave.

11

5, 18

Dorchester St.

11

45

41, 46

1, 47

8, 10

Columbus Ave.

46

22, 23, 45

Dudley Sq.

15, 45

Southampton St.

5, 18

Columbus Park

ROXBURY

Washington Park

Warren St.

45

Dudley St.

15

9

18

McCormack Housing

Dorchester Bay

22, 29, 44

28

44

14, 19, 23, 28

Dudley St.

19

Edward Everett Square

18

17

Mt. Vernon St.

16

UMass Boston

Washington St.

Seaver St.

44

Blue Hill Ave.

22, 29

Grove Hall

Columbia Rd.

Kane Square

17

18, 19

16

Franklin Park

28

45

Peabody Loop

Morton St.

21, 31

16

Ronan Park

Geneva Ave.

15, 17, 19

Washington St.

19

18

20, 210

20, 210

Adams St.

rest Hills Cemetery

American Legion Hwy.

Blue Hill Ave.

Talbot Ave.

22

Franklin Field

22

Franklin Field

29

23, 28

18

Neponset Ave.

1 mile

1.5 km

DORCHESTER

MAP 23 Commuter Rail Lines & Outer (T) Stops

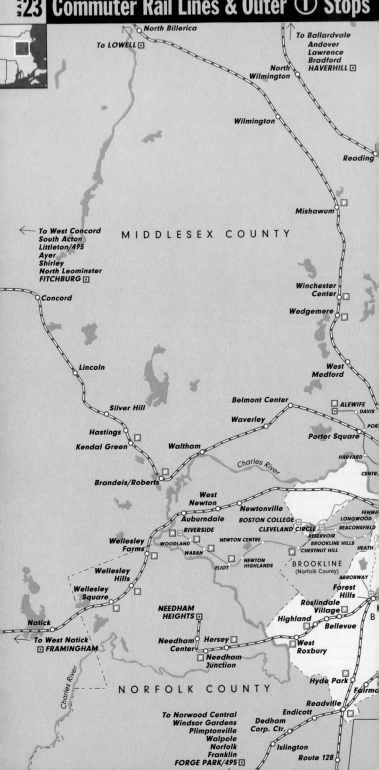

North Billerica
To LOWELL 🔲

To Ballardvale
Andover
Lawrence
Bradford
HAVERHILL 🔲

North Wilmington

Wilmington

Reading

Mishawum

MIDDLESEX COUNTY

To West Concord
South Acton
Littleton/495
Ayer
Shirley
North Leominster
FITCHBURG 🔲

Concord

Winchester Center

Wedgemere

Lincoln

West Medford

Silver Hill

Belmont Center

Waverley

ALEWIFE
DAVIS
POR

Hastings
Kendal Green

Waltham

Porter Square

HARVARD

Brandeis/Roberts

CENTR.

Charles River

West Newton

Newtonville

Auburndale

BOSTON COLLEGE

CLEVELAND CIRCLE

FENWA
LONGWOOD
BEACONSFIELD

RIVERSIDE

Wellesley Farms

WOODLAND

WABAN

NEWTON CENTRE

RESERVOIR
BROOKLINE HILLS
CHESTNUT HILL
HEATH

Wellesley Hills

ELIOT

NEWTON HIGHLANDS

BROOKLINE
(Norfolk County)

ARBORWAY

Wellesley Square

Forest Hills

Natick

Roslindale Village

To West Natick
🔲 FRAMINGHAM

NEEDHAM HEIGHTS 🔲

Highland

Bellevue

B

Needham Center

Hersey

West Roxbury

Needham Junction

Charles River

NORFOLK COUNTY

Hyde Park

Fairmo

Readville

Endicott

To Norwood Central
Windsor Gardens
Plimptonville
Walpole
Norfolk
Franklin
FORGE PARK/495 🔲

Dedham Corp. Ctr.

Islington

Route 128

MAP
23

North Beverly

To Hamilton/
Wenham
◻ IPSWICH

To Montserrat
Prides Crossing
Beverly Farms
Manchester-by-
the-Sea
West Gloucester
Gloucester
ROCKPORT ◻

Beverly
Depot

ESSEX COUNTY

Wakefield

Greenwood

Salem

Swampscott

Melrose/Highlands

Lynn

Melrose/
Cedar Park

Wyoming Hill

OAK
GROVE

Lynn
Harbor

Nahant
Bay

MALDEN
CENTER

Malden
Center

ATLANTIC
OCEAN

ELLINGTON

WONDERLAND

Chelsea

REVERE BEACH

BEACHMONT

SULLIVAN

SUFFOLK DOWNS

ORIENT HEIGHTS

WOOD ISLAND

LECHMERE

AIRPORT

NORTH
STATION

MAVERICK

KENDALL

Logan
International
Airport

Yawkey

SOUTH
STATION

Back
Bay

BROADWAY

Boston
Harbor

ANDREW

Ruggles

JFK/
U MASS

SUFFOLK COUNTY

SAVIN HILL

Uphams
Corner

FOREST
HILLS

FIELDS
CORNER

SHAWMUT

TON

ASHMONT

Morton
Street

CEDAR GROVE

BUTLER
MILTON

Quincy
Bay

VALLEY RD

CAPEN ST

NORTH QUINCY

MATTAPAN

WOLLASTON

N

QUINCY CENTER

NORFOLK COUNTY

PLYMOUTH
COUNTY

To Canton Jct
Canton Center
STOUGHTON ◻
Sharon
Mansfield
Attleboro
South Attleboro

QUINCY ADAMS

KEY

Commuter Rail
Lines & Stations

● Open during baseball
season

MBTA RAPID TRANSIT (T)
○— Red Line
○— Blue Line
○— Orange Line
○— Green Line
◻ End of Line
◻ MBTA Parking

0 ——————— 4 miles
0 ——————— 6 kms

MAP **24** **Top Attractions**

Hurley St.
Charles St.
Spring St.
Bent St.
Cambridgeside
Galleria
Rogers St.
Binney St.
Binney St.
Munroe St.
Markel St.
Windsor St.
Bristol St.
Clark St.
Cardinal Medeiros Ave.
Fulkerson St.
3rd St.
2nd St.
1st St.
Edwin Land Blvd.
Cambridge Pkwy.

Washington St.
Portland St.
Broadway
Potter St.
Athenaeum St.

CAMBRIDGE

Allen Dr.
Main St.
Massachusetts Ave.
Osban St.

Longfellow Br.

Albany St.
Vossar St.
Ames St.
Amherst St.
Carleton
MIT
(2A)

Kresge Auditorium
Memorial Dr.
Harvard Br.
(3)

Briggs Field (MIT)

Charles River

Hatch Band Shell

N

0   1200 feet
0   400 meters

James J. Storrow Memorial Dr.
Beacon St.
Back St.
Marlborough St.
Berkeley St.

Bay State Rd.
Back St.
Raleigh St.
(20)
1
Kenmore Sq.
Beacon St.
Newbury St.
(90)
Ipswich St.
Charlesgate E.
Charlesgate W.
Hereford St.
Gloucester St.
Fairfield St.
Commonwealth Ave.
Exeter St.
Dartmouth St.
Clarendon St.
10
Newbury St.
Boylston St.
11
Blagden St.
12 **13**
14
(90)
Back Bay Station
(28)

Brookline Ave.
Lansdowne St.
Ipswich St.
2
Hynes Convention Center
Prudential Center
Dalton St.
Belvidere St.
Copley Place
(9)

Van
Ness St.
Yawkey Wy.
Jersey St.
Back Bay Fens Park
Burbank St.
Westland Ave.
Massachusetts Ave.
Huntington Ave.
St. Botolph St.
Carleton St.
Warren Ave.
Pembroke St.
W. Newton St.
Montgomery Park
W. Canton St.

Boylston St.
Kilmarnock St.
Peterborough St.
Queensberry St.
Agassiz Rd.
St. Stephen St.
7
6
Columbus Ave.
Concord Sq.
Rutland St.
Rutland Sq.
Tremont St.
Worcester St.
Newland St.
Shawmut Ave.

Park Dr.
Hemenway St.
Forsyth Fwy.
Forsyth St.
Gainsborough St.
Massachusetts Ave.

4
5
8
9
Museum Rd.
Louis Prang St.
Huntington Ave.
3

Listed by Site Number

1 Boston University	**7** Christian Science Headquarters	**14** John Hancock Tower Observatory
2 Fenway Park	**8** Franklin Park Zoo	**15** Public Garden (Swan Boats)
3 Isabella Stewart Gardner Museum	**9** Arnold Arboretum	**16** Bull & Finch Pub (Cheers)
4 Museum of Fine Arts	**10** Newbury Street	**17** Wang Center
5 Northeastern University	**11** Boston Public Library	**18** Chinatown
6 Symphony Hall	**12** Copley Square	
	13 Trinity Church	

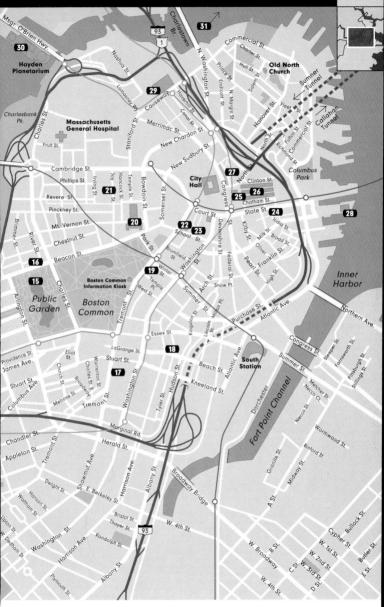

MAP 24

Listed by Site Number (cont.)

MAP 25 Freedom Trail & Black Heritage Trail

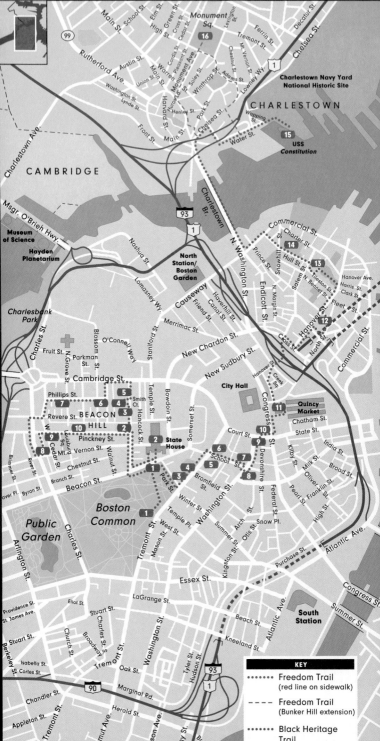

KEY

······· Freedom Trail
(red line on sidewalk)

– – – Freedom Trail
(Bunker Hill extension)

······· Black Heritage
Trail

MAP 25

Listed by Site Number

Freedom Trail

1 Boston Common
2 State House
3 Park St Church
4 Granary Burying Ground
5 King's Chapel
6 First Public School
7 Old Corner Bookstore
8 Old South Meeting House
9 Old State House
10 Boston Massacre Site
12 Paul Revere House
11 Faneuil Hall
13 Old North Church

14 Copp's Hill Burying Ground
15 USS *Constitution*
16 Bunker Hill Monument

Black Heritage Trail

1 Robert Gould Shaw Memorial
2 George Middleton House
3 Abiel Smith School
4 African Meeting House
5 Smith Court Residences
6 Coburn's Gaming House

7 Lewis Hayden House
8 Charles St Meeting House
9 John J Smith House
10 Phillips School

Listed Alphabetically

FREEDOM TRAIL (☎ 242-5642)

Boston Massacre Site, 10.
State & Devonshire Sts

Boston Common, 1. Park St

Bunker Hill Monument, 16.
Monument Sq, Charlestown

Copp's Hill Burying Ground, 14.
Charter St

Faneuil Hall, 11.
Faneuil Hall Marketplace

First Public School, 5. School St

Granary Burying Ground, 4.
Tremont & Park Sts

King's Chapel, 6. 58 Tremont St

Old Corner Bookstore, 7. 3 School St

Old North Church, 13. 193 Salem St

Old South Meeting House, 8.
310 Washington St

Old State House, 9.
206 Washington St

Park St Church, 3. 1 Park St

Paul Revere House, 12. 19 North Sq

State House, 2. One Ashburton Pl

USS *Constitution*, 15.
Constitution Wharf, Charlestown

BLACK HERITAGE TRAIL
(☎ 742-5415)

Abiel Smith School, 3. 46 Joy St

African Meeting House, 4.
8 Smith Court

Charles St Meeting House, 8.
Mt Vernon & Charles Sts

Coburn's Gaming House, 6.
2 Phillips St

George Middleton House, 2.
5-7 Pinckney St

John J Smith House, 9. 86 Pinckney St

Lewis Hayden House, 7. 66 Phillips St

Phillips School, 10.
Anderson & Pinckney Sts

Robert Gould Shaw Memorial, 1.
Beacon & Park Sts

Smith Court Residences, 5.
3-10 Smith Court

MAP 26 Architecture

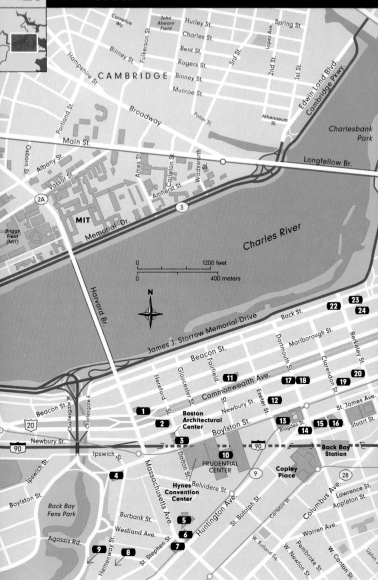

Listed by Site Number

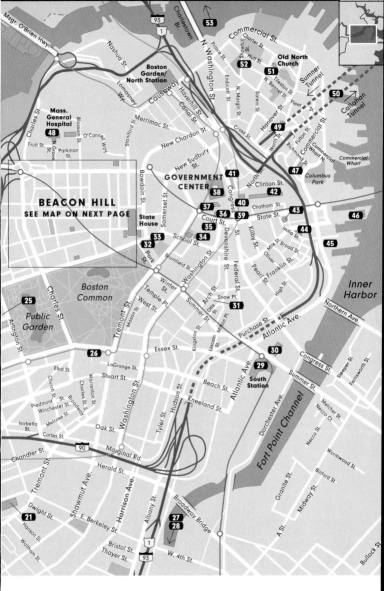

MAP 26

Msgr. O'Brien Hwy.

Charlestown Br.

53

Commercial St.

Charter St.

Prince St.

Hull St.

Old North Church

52

51

N. Bennet St.

Tileston St.

Sumner Tunnel

50

Callahan Tunnel

Nashua St.

N. Washington St.

Endicott St.

N. Margin St.

Salem St.

Hanover St.

North St.

Fleet St.

Boston Garden/ North Station

Causeway

Haverhill St.

Canal St.

Cross St.

49

Fulton St.

Richmond St.

Commercial St.

Commercial Wharf

Commercial Wharf

Lomasney Wy.

Merrimac St.

47

Columbus Park

Mass. General Hospital

48

Blossom St.

O'Connel Way

Stanford St.

New Chardon St.

N. Grove

Fruit St.

Parkman St.

New Sudbury St.

41

Northern St.

Clinton St.

42

46

Bowdoin St.

GOVERNMENT CENTER

38

40

Chatham St.

43

BEACON HILL

SEE MAP ON NEXT PAGE

Somerset St.

37

36

39

State St.

India St.

44

Court St.

35

Kilby St.

Milk St.

Broad St.

45

State House

33

School St.

34

Devonshire St.

Oliver St.

Bromfield St.

Federal St.

Franklin St.

Inner Harbor

32

Park St.

Washington St.

Arch St.

Pearl St.

High St.

Boston Common

Winter St.

Temple Pl.

Snow Pl.

31

West St.

Summer St.

Purchase St.

25

Charles St.

Tremont St.

Mason St.

Avery St.

Lincoln St.

Kingston St.

Atlantic Ave.

Atlantic Ave.

Northern Ave.

Public Garden

Arlington St.

26

Essex St.

LaGrange St.

Stuart St.

Beach St.

South Station

30

29

Congress St.

Summer St.

Sleeper St.

Farnsworth St.

Eliot St.

Church St.

Charles St. S.

Warrenton St.

Piedmont St.

Winchester St.

Broadway

Melrose St.

Washington St.

Hudson St.

Tyler St.

Kneeland St.

Dorchester Ave.

Fort Point Channel

Melcher St.

Necco Ct.

Necco St.

Wormwood St.

Isabella St.

Cortes St.

Oak St.

Granite St.

Binford St.

Midway St.

Chandler St.

90

Marginal Rd.

Tremont St.

Shawmut Ave.

Herald St.

A St.

Dwight St.

21

E. Berkeley St.

Harrison Ave.

Albany St.

Broadway Bridge

27

28

Wormwood St.

Hanson St.

Waltham St.

Bristol St.

Thayer St.

1

93

W. 4th St.

Bullock St.

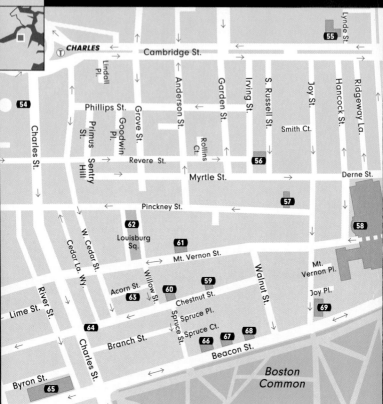

Architecture 26

MAP 27 **Outdoor Statuary**

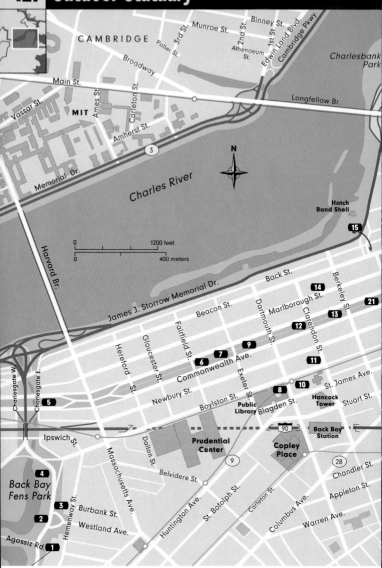

Listed by Site Number

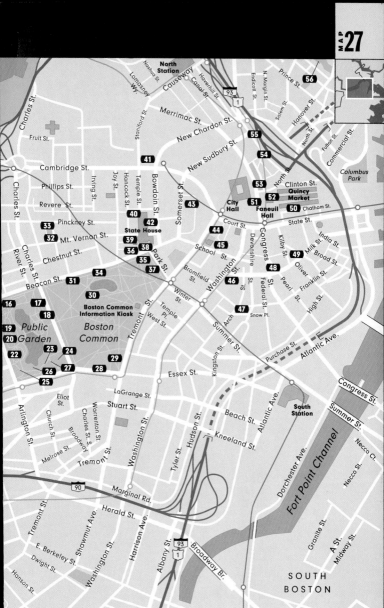

MAP **27**

MAP 28 **Churches and Cemeteries**

8

99 Rutherford

SOMERVILLE

Linwood St.
Joy St.
Medford St.
28

93

Winter St.
Gore St.
Cambridge St.
Otis St.
6
7
28
Bershire St.
Marney St.
James Wy.
8th St.
7th St.
6th St.
5th St.
Sciarappa St.
Thorndike St.
Spring St.
Msgr. O'Brien Hwy.
York St.
Cornelius Wy.
Cardinal Medeiros Ave.
Fulkerson St.
John Ahearn Field
Hurley St.
Charles St.
Bent St.
3rd St.
2nd St.
Lopez Ave.
1st St.
Museum of Science
Hayden Planetarium
Binney St.
Rogers St.
Binney St.
Munroe St.
CAMBRIDGE
Charlesbank Park
Charles St.
Blossom St.
O'Connell
Mass General Hospital

1
2
3
4
5
Potter St.
Broadway
Athenaeum St.
Edwin Land Blvd.
Cambridge Pkwy.
Longfellow Br.
Fruit St.
N Grove St.
Parkman St.
Cambridge St.
Phillips St.
Anderson St.
Irving St.
Garden St.

Vassar St.
Ames St.
Carleton St.
Amherst St.
Wadsworth St.
Main St.
3
MIT
Memorial Dr.
N
Revere St.
Pinckney St.
W. Cedar St.
Chestnut St.
Walnut St.
23

Charles River
Harvard Br.
0   1200 feet
0   400 meters
Hatch Band Shell
Beaver Pl.
Byron St.
Beacon St.
Brimmer St.
River St.
Boston Common

James J. Storrow Memorial Drive
Back St.
Beacon St.
Marlborough St.
Berkeley St.
Arlington St.
Public Garden
Charles St.
24

20
Commonwealth Ave.
Fairfield St.
Exeter St.
Dartmouth St.
Clarendon St.
18
19
21
22
Providence St.
St. James Ave.
Eliot St.
Stuart St.
Charlesgate E.
Hereford St.
Gloucester St.
Newbury St.
16
17
Boylston St.
Blagden St.
Stuart St.
Church St.
Broadway
Tremont St.
11
12
Public Library
Hynes Convention Center
90
Copley Place
Back Bay Station
Isabella St.
Cortes St.
Ipswich St.
Dalton St.
Prudential Center
9
Chandler St.
Belvidere St.
Christian Science Center
Huntington Ave.
Carleton St.
Columbus Ave.
28
Lawrence St.
Appleton St.
Tremont St.
Hanson St.
Waltham St.
E. Berkeley St.
Shawmut Ave.

Back Bay Fens Park
13
St. Botolph St.
W. Rutland Sq.
Warren Ave.
W. Canton St.
W. Dedham St.
Dwight St.
Burbank St.
Westland Ave.
Massachusetts Ave.
Symphony Hall
Wellington St.
Gainsborough St.
W. Newton St.
Rutland Sq.
Rutland St.
W. Concord St.
Pembroke St.
Shawmut Ave.
Washington St.
Upton St.
15
Msgr. Reynolds Wy.

Hemenway St.
St. Stephen St.
Forsyth St.
Northeastern University
Columbus Ave.
Tremont St.
Camden St.
Northampton St.
Massachusetts Ave.
W. Springfield St.
W. Worcester St.
Newland St.
Blackstone Sq.
Franklin Sq.
14
Harrison Ave.
E. Canton St.
Plymouth St.
E. Dedham St.
Randolph
Albany

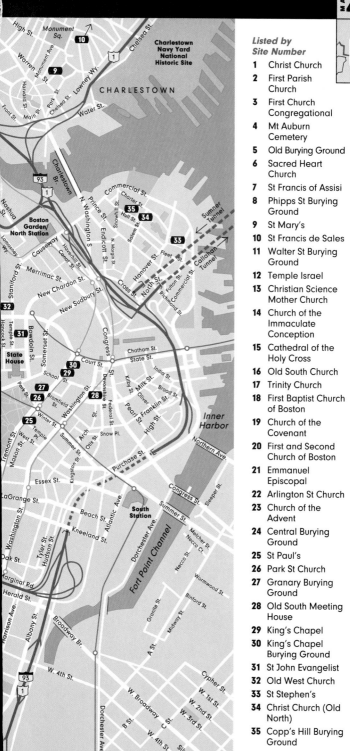

MAP 28

CHARLESTOWN

Charlestown
Navy Yard
National
Historic Site

Charlestown Navy Yard National Historic Site

Boston
Garden/
North Station

State
House

South
Station

Inner
Harbor

Fort Point Channel

Listed Alphabetically

CHURCHES

Arlington St Church, 22.
351 Boylston St
☎ 536-7050. Unitarian.

Cathedral of the Holy Cross, 15.
1400 Washington St
☎ 542-5682. Catholic.

Christ Church, 1. Garden St,
Cambridge ☎ 876-0200. Episcopal.

Christ Church (Old North), 34.
193 Salem St ☎ 523-6676. Episcopal.

**Christian Science Mother
Church, 13.** 175 Huntington Ave
☎ 450-2000.

Church of the Advent, 23.
30 Brimmer St ☎ 523-2377. Episcopal.

Church of the Covenant, 19.
67 Newbury St
☎ 266-7480. Presbyterian.

**Church of the Immaculate
Conception, 14.** 775 Harrison St
☎ 536-8440. Catholic.

Emmanuel Episcopal, 21.
15 Newbury St ☎ 536-3355.

First Baptist Church of Boston, 18.
110 Commonwealth Ave ☎ 267-3148.

**First and Second Church of
Boston, 20.** 66 Marlborough St
☎ 267-6730. Unitarian.

First Church Congregational, 3.
11 Garden St, Cambridge ☎ 876-5829.

First Parish Church, 2. 3 Church St,
Cambridge ☎ 876-7772. Unitarian.

King's Chapel, 29. 58 Tremont St
☎ 523-1749. Unitarian.

Old South Church, 16.
645 Boylston St
☎ 536-1970. Church of Christ.

Old South Meeting House, 28.
310 Washington St ☎ 482-6349.

Old West Church, 32.
131 Cambridge St
☎ 227-5088. Methodist.

Park St Church, 26. 1 Park St
☎ 523-3383. Congregational.

Sacred Heart Church, 6. 49 Sixth St,
Cambridge ☎ 547-0399. Catholic.

St Francis de Sales, 10.
325 Bunker Hill, Charlestown
☎ 242-4426. Catholic.

St Francis of Assisi, 7.
42 Sciarappa St, Cambridge
☎ 876-6754. Catholic.

St John Evangelist, 31.
35 Bowdoin St ☎ 227-5242. Episcopal.

St Mary's, 9. 46 Winthrop St,
Charlestown
☎ 242-2196. Catholic.

St Paul's, 25. 138 Tremont St
☎ 482-5800. Episcopal.

St Stephen's, 33. 24 Clark St
☎ 523-1230. Catholic.

Temple Israel, 12. 260 Riverway
☎ 566-3960. Jewish.

Trinity Church, 17. Copley Square
☎ 536-0944. Episcopal.

CEMETERIES

Central Burying Ground, 24.
Tremont St/Boston Common

Copp's Hill Burying Ground, 35.
Charter St

Granary Burying Ground, 27. Park &
Tremont Sts

King's Chapel Burying Ground, 30.
58 Tremont St

Mt Auburn Cemetery, 4.
Mt Auburn St, Cambridge

**Old Burying Ground (First Parish
Church), 5.** Garden St, Cambridge

Phipps St Burying Ground, 8.
Phipps St, Charlestown

Walter St Burying Ground, 11.
Arnold Arboretum, Roslindale

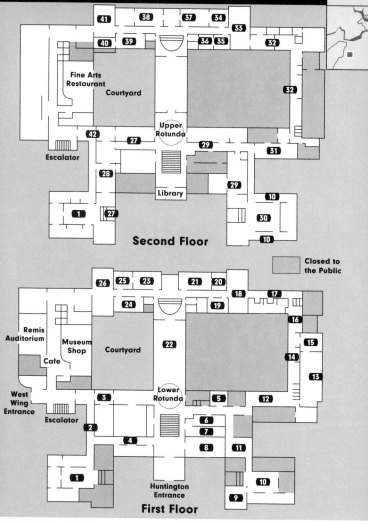

Second Floor

First Floor

Closed to the Public

Listed by Site Number

1 Japanese Art
2 Islamic Art
3 Brown Gallery
4 Indian Art
5 Egyptian Mummies
6 Graphics
7 Musical Instruments
8 Nubian Art
9 Etruscan Art
10 Greek Art
11 Near-Eastern Art
12 18th-C Amer Furn
13 18th-C French Art
14 18th-C Boston
15 English Silver

16 19th-C American
17 American Federal
18 Copley & Contemp
19 American Neo-Classic & Romantic
20 Amer Folk Painting
21 19th-C Landscape
22 American Modern
23 American Masters
24 Early 20th-C
25 Amer Impressionism
26 20th-C Amer & Euro
27 Chinese Art
28 Bernat Galleries
29 Egyptian Art

30 Roman Art
31 Medieval Art
32 European Decorative Arts
33 Impressionism
34 19th-C French & Eng
35 Post-Impressionism
36 Coolidge Collection
37 18th-C Italian
38 Dutch & Flemish Art
39 Renaissance
40 Spanish Chapel
41 Baroque Art
42 Himalayan Art

MAP **30** **Museums/Downtown**

CAMBRIDGE

Gore St.
Cambridge St.
Elm St.
Columbia St.
Windsor St.
Willow St.
Berkshire St.
Donnelly Field
Marney James Wy.
8th St.
7th St.
Otis St.
Thorndike St.
Hampshire St.
Market St.
Bristol St.
Clark St.
Cardinal Medeiros Ave.
Binney St.
Fulkerson St.
Hurley St.
Charles St.
Bent St.
Rogers St.
Binney St.
Munroe St.
Potter St.
3rd St.
2nd St.
1st St.
Spring St.
Edwin Land Blvd.
Cambridge Pkwy.
Athenaeum St.

Washington St.
Broadway
Portland St.
Allen Dr.
Main St.
Osborn St.
Massachusetts Ave.
Vassar St.
MIT
Albany St.
2A
Amherst St.
Ames St.
Carleton St.
Memorial Dr.
Longfellow Br.
Harvard Br.

Briggs Field (MIT)

Charles River

N

0   1200 feet
0   400 meters

James J. Storrow Memorial Dr.
Back St.
Beacon St.
Marlborough St.
Berkeley St.
Dartmouth St.
Clarendon St.
Fairfield St.
Gloucester St.
Hereford St.
Commonwealth Ave.
Exeter St.
Newbury St.
Boylston St.
Blagden St.

Bay State Rd.
Back St.
Raleigh St.
Deerfield St.
Charlesgate W.
Charlesgate E.
Kenmore Sq.
20
Beacon St.
90
Newbury St.
Lansdowne St.
Ipswich St.
Brookline Ave.
Fenway Park
Ipswich St.
Yawkey Way
Van Ness St.
Boylston St.
Jersey St.
Peterborough St.
Kilmarnock St.
Queensberry St.
Park Dr.
Back Bay Fens Park
Agassiz Rd.
Burbank St.
Westland Ave.
St. Stephen St.
Forsyth Pl.
Forsyth St.
Hemenway St.
Symphony Hall
Gainsborough St.
Huntington Ave.
Northeastern University
Massachusetts Ave.
Dalton St.
Belvidere St.
PRUDENTIAL CENTER
9
Massachusetts Ave.
Christian Science Center
St. Botolph St.
Huntington Ave.
COPLEY PLACE
28
Carleton St.
Warren Ave.
Columbus Ave.
Newton St.
Pembroke St.
Rutland Sq.
Concord Sq.
Tremont St.
Rutland St.
Worcester St.
Newland St.
Shawmut Ave.
W. Canton St.
Montgomery Park

90
Ipswich St.
7
8

1
2
3
9
4
5
6

Listed by Site Number

1 MIT/Hart Nautical	**5** Museum of Fine Arts	**9** Gibson House
2 Hayden Gallery/MIT	**6** Mapparium/ Christian Science	**10** Children's Museum
3 Sports Museum of New England	**7** Inst of Contemp Art	**11** Boston Tea Party Mus
4 Gardner Museum	**8** Boston Public Library	**12** Old South Meeting House

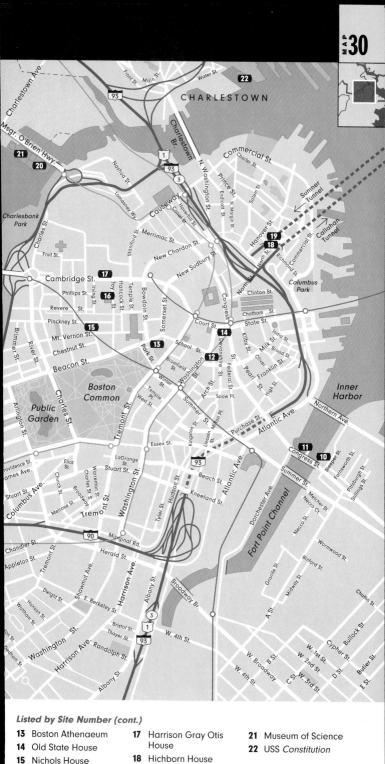

MAP 30

CHARLESTOWN

Charlestown Ave.

Msgr. O'Brien Hwy.

21
20

Front St.   Main St.   Water St.   **22**

Charlestown Br.

N. Washington St.

Commercial St.

Charter St.

Charlesbank Park

Charles St.

Nashua St.

Lomasney Wy.

P.I. Burroughs

Fruit St.

Causeway

Haverhill St.

Canal St.

Prince St.

Endicott St.

Merrimac St.

New Chardon St.

New Sudbury St.

N. Margin St.

Salem St.

Hanover St.

19
18

Richmond

North St.

Sumner Tunnel

Callahan Tunnel

Commercial St.

Columbus Park

Cambridge St.   **17**

Phillips St.

Revere   St.

Pinckney St.

15

Mt. Vernon St.

Chestnut St.

Beacon St.

Irving St.

Temple St.

Hancock St.

Joy St.

16

Bowdoin St.

Somerset St.

Park St.

13

Cambridge St.

Clinton St.

Congress St.

Chatham   St.

State St.

Court St.   **14**

School   St.

Bromfield St.

Washington

12

Winter   St.

Temple Pl.

West St.

Devonshire   St.

Federal St.

Arch St.

Summer   St.

Snow Pl.

Kilby St.

India St.

Milk St.   Broad St.

Oliver   St.

Pearl   St.

Franklin St.

High St.

Inner Harbor

Brimmer   St.

River St.

Charles St.

Boston Common

Public Garden

Arlington St.

Tremont St.

Essex St.

Beacon St.

Kingston St.

Lincoln St.

Milton Pl.

Purchase St.

Atlantic Ave.

Northern Ave.

11
10

Congress St.

Sleeper St.

Farnsworth St.

Pittsburgh St.

Stillings St.

Providence St.
James Ave.

Eliot
Church.

St.
St.

LaGrange St.

Stuart St.

Warrenton St.

Charles St.

Melrose St.

Broadway

Stuart St.

Columbus Ave.

Tremont St.

Washington St.

Beach St.

Kneeland St.

Atlantic Ave.

Dorchester Ave.

Summer St.

Fort Point Channel

Melcher St.

Necco Ct.

Necco St.

Wormwood St.

Chandler St.

Appleton St.

Tremont St.

Shawmut Ave.

Dwight St.

Hanson St.

Waltham St.

E. Berkeley St.

Harrison Ave.

Hudson St.

Tyler St.

Marginal Rd.

Herald St.

Albany St.

Broadway Br.

Binford St.

Granite St.

Midway St.

A St.

B. St.

W. 1st St.

W. 2nd St.

C St.

W. 3rd St.

D St.

E. St.

Chaffin St.

Cypher St.

Bullock St.

Butler St.

Washington

Harrison Ave.

Bristol St.

Thayer St.

Randolph St.

Albany St.

W. 4th St.

W. Broadway

W. 4th St.

MAP 30 Museums/Greater Boston

Listed by Site Number

23 Somerville Museum

24 Longfellow National Historic Site

25 University Museum

26 Peabody Museum/ Harvard

27 Sackler Museum

28 Fogg Art Museum

29 Busch-Reisinger

30 DeCordova Museum

31 Kennedy National Historic Site

32 Longyear Museum & Historical Society

33 Museum of Transportation

34 Museum of Afro-American Artists

35 Kennedy Library

36 Commonwealth Mus

37 Blue Hills Trailside

Listed Alphabetically

Blue Hills Trailside, 37.
1904 Canton Ave, Milton
☎ 333-0690

Boston Athenaeum, 13.
10 1/2 Beacon St
☎ 227-0270

Boston Public Library, 8.
666 Boylston St
☎ 536-5400

Boston Tea Party Museum, 11.
Congress St Bridge
☎ 338-1773

Busch-Reisinger, 29. 32 Quincy St
☎ 495-2338

Children's Museum, 10.
300 Congress St
☎ 426-8855

Commonwealth Museum, 36.
220 Morrissey Blvd
☎ 727-9268

DeCordova Museum, 30.
51 Sandy Pond Rd, Lincoln
☎ 259-8355

Fogg Art Museum, 28.
32 Quincy St, Cambridge
☎ 495-9400

Gibson House, 9. 137 Beacon St
☎ 267-6338

Harrison Gray Otis House, 17.
141 Cambridge St
☎ 227-3956

Hayden Gallery/MIT, 2.
160 Memorial Dr, Cambridge
☎ 253-4680

Hayden Planetarium, 20.
Science Park
☎ 723-2500

Hichborn House, 18. 19 North Square
☎ 523-1676

Institute of Contemporary Art, 7.
955 Boylston St
☎ 266-5151

**Isabella Stewart Gardner
Museum, 4.** 280 Fenway
☎ 566-1401

Kennedy Library, 35.
Columbia Pt, Dorchester
☎ 929-4500

Kennedy National Historic Site, 31.
83 Beals St, Brookline
☎ 566-7937

**Longfellow National Historic
Site, 24.** 105 Brattle St, Cambridge
☎ 876-4491

**Longyear Museum &
Historical Society, 32.**
120 Seaver St, Brookline
☎ 277-8943

Mapparium/Christian Sci, 6.
Norway St & Mass Ave
☎ 450-2000

MIT/Hart Nautical, 1.
265 Mass Ave, Cambridge
☎ 253-5942

Museum of Afro-Amer Artists, 34.
300 Walnut Ave, Roxbury
☎ 442-8614

**Museum of Afro-American
History, 16.** 46 Joy St
☎ 742-1854

Museum of Fine Arts, 5.
465 Huntington Ave
☎ 267-9300

Museum of Science, 21.
Science Park
☎ 723-2500

Museum of Transportation, 33.
15 Newton St, Brookline
☎ 522-6140

Nichols House, 15. 55 Mt Vernon St
☎ 227-6993

Old South Meeting House, 12.
310 Washington St
☎ 482-6439

Old State House, 14.
206 Washington St
☎ 720-3290

Paul Revere House, 19.
19 North Square
☎ 523-2338

Peabody Museum/Harvard, 26.
11 Divinity Ave, Cambridge
☎ 495-2248

Sackler Museum, 27.
485 Broadway at Quincy St,
Cambridge ☎ 495-9400

Somerville Museum, 23.
1 Westwood Rd, Somerville
☎ 666-9810

Sports Museum of New England, 3.
Cambridgeside Galleria, Cambridge
☎ 577-7678

University Museum, 25.
24 Oxford St, Cambridge
☎ 495-1910

USS *Constitution*, 22.
Constitution Wharf, Charlestown
☎ 426-1812

MAP 31 Art Galleries/Newbury Street

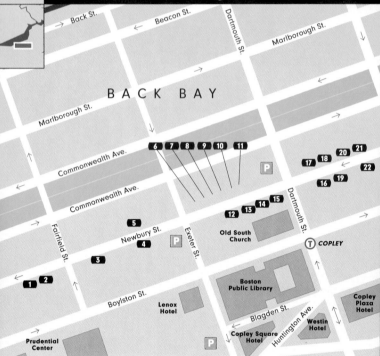

Listed by Site Number

1 Iguana Gallery
2 Kanegis Gallery
3 Vose Galleries
4 Crane Collection
5 Newman Gallery Ltd
6 Nielsen Gallery
7 Society Arts & Crafts
8 Chase Gallery
9 Pucker Gallery
10 Childs Gallery
11 Marlborough Galleries
12 Wenniger Graphic
13 Guild of Boston
14 Copley Society of Boston
14 Walker Alfred
15 Newbury Art Studio
16 Dyansen
17 Arden Gallery
18 Galerie Europeene
18 Randall Beck
19 Judi Rotenburg
20 Gallerie Mouriat

Listed Alphabetically

Alpha Gallery, 27. 14 Newbury St
☎ 536-4465

Arden Gallery, 17. 129 Newbury St
☎ 247-0610

Barbara Krakow Gallery, 29.
10 Newbury St ☎ 262-4490

Bloch Gallery, 22. 116 Newbury St
☎ 266-5575

Bronte Contemporary Arts, 24.
32 Newbury St ☎ 236-0058

Chase Gallery, 8. 173 Newbury St
☎ 859-7222

Childs Gallery, 10. 169 Newbury St
☎ 266-1108

Copley Society of Boston, 14.
158 Newbury St ☎ 536-5049

Crane Collection, 4. 218 Newbury St
☎ 262-4080

Dyansen, 16. 132A Newbury St
☎ 262-4800

Galerie Europeene, 18.
123 Newbury St ☎ 859-7062

Gallerie Mouriat, 20. 119 Newbury St
☎ 536-1177

Guild of Boston Artists, 13.
162 Newbury St ☎ 536-7660

Haley & Steele, 23. 91 Newbury St
☎ 536-6339

Iguana Gallery, 1. 246 Newbury St
☎ 247-0211

Judi Rotenburg, 19. 130 Newbury St
☎ 437-1518

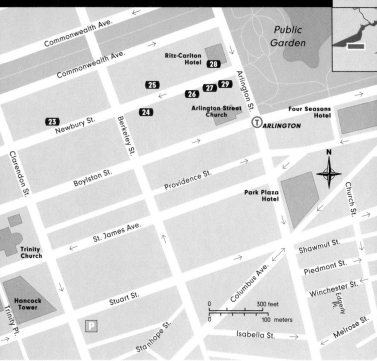

MAP 31

MAP 32 Exploring Cambridge

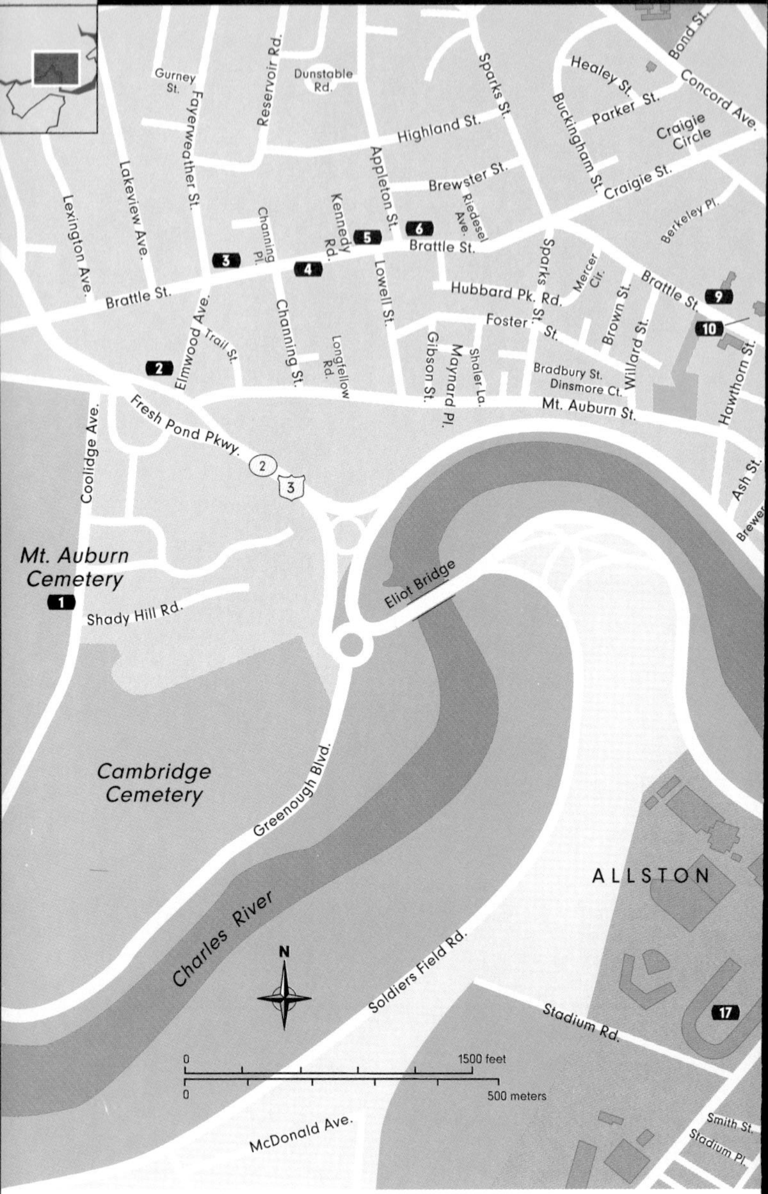

Gurney St.
Fayerweather St.
Reservoir Rd.
Dunstable Rd.
Sparks St.
Healey St.
Bond St.
Concord Ave.
Parker St.
Buckingham St.
Craigie Circle
Highland St.
Appleton St.
Brewster St.
Craigie St.
Lakeview Ave.
Lexington Ave.
Channing Pl.
Kennedy Rd.
Riedesel Ave.
Berkeley Pl.
Brattle St.
Lowell St.
Hubbard Pk. Rd.
Mercer Cir.
Brown St.
Willard St.
Foster St.
Elmwood Ave.
Trail St.
Channing St.
Longfellow Rd.
Gibson St.
Maynard Pl.
Shaler La.
Bradbury St.
Dinsmore Ct.
Hawthorn St.
Mt. Auburn St.
Coolidge Ave.
Fresh Pond Pkwy.
2
3
Ash St.
Mt. Auburn Cemetery
Shady Hill Rd.
Eliot Bridge
Cambridge Cemetery
Greenough Blvd.
ALLSTON
Charles River
N
Soldiers Field Rd.
Stadium Rd.
0
1500 feet
0
500 meters
McDonald Ave.
Smith St.
Stadium Pl.
1
2
3
4
5
6
9
10
17

Listed by Site Number

1 Mt Auburn Cemetery
2 Elmwood House
3 Fayerweather House
4 Brattle Street (Tory Row)
5 Hooper House
6 Thomas Lee House
7 Asa Gray House
8 Richards House
9 Longfellow National Historic Site
10 Oliver Hastings House
11 Stoughton House
12 First Church Congregational
13 Radcliffe College
14 Dexter Pratt House
15 Christ Church
16 Brattle House
17 Harvard Stadium
18 Old Burying Ground
19 Dawes Island
20 Massachusetts Hall
21 Boylston Hall

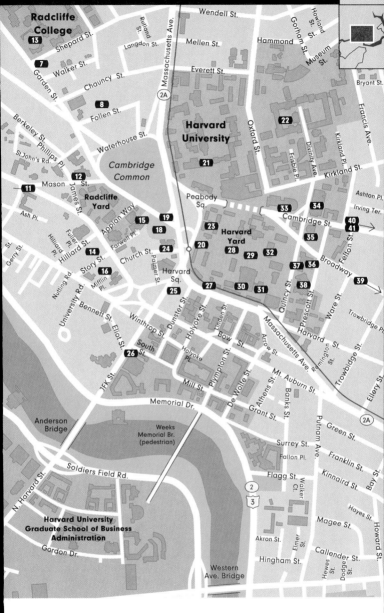

MAP **32** **Exploring Cambridge**

Listed Alphabetically

Arthur M. Sackler Museum, 35. 485 Broadway ☎ 495-9400

Asa Gray House, 7. 88 Garden St

Boylston Hall, 21. Harvard Yard

Brattle House, 16. 42 Brattle St ☎ 547-6789

Brattle Street (Tory Row), 4.

Busch-Reisinger Museum, 37. 32 Quincy St ☎ 495-2317

Cambridge Discovery Booth, 25. Zero Harvard Square ☎ 497-1630

Carpenter Visual Arts, 38. Prescott St

Christ Church, 15. Zero Garden St ☎ 876-0200

Dawes Island, 19. Garden St

Dexter Pratt House, 14. 56 Brattle St ☎ 547-6789

Elmwood House, 2. 33 Elmwood Ave

Fayerweather House, 3. 175 Brattle St

First Church Congregational, 12. 11 Garden St ☎ 876-5829

First Parish Church, 24. 3 Church St ☎ 876-7772

Fogg Art Museum, 36. 32 Quincy St ☎ 495-9400

Fuller House, 39. 71 Cherry St

Gund Hall, 34. Quincy St

Harvard Museums of Cultural and Natural History, 22. 26 Oxford St ☎ 495-3045

Harvard Stadium, 17. N Harvard St & Soldiers Field Rd ☎ 495-2211

Harvard Yard, 29. Harvard Square

Holden Chapel, 23. Harvard Yard

Hooper House, 5. 159 Brattle St

John Hicks House, 26. 64 JFK St

Longfellow National Historic Site, 9. 105 Brattle St ☎ 876-4491

Massachusetts Hall, 20. Harvard Yard

Memorial Hall, 33. Harvard Yard

Mt Auburn Cemetery, 1. Mt Auburn St ☎ 547-7105

Old Burying Ground, 18. Massachusetts Ave & Church St ☎ 876-7772

Oliver Hastings House, 10. 101 Brattle St

Pusey Library, 31. Harvard Yard

Radcliffe College, 13. 10 Garden St ☎ 495-8601

Richards House, 8. 15 Follen St

Sacred Heart Church, 40. 49 Sixth St ☎ 547-0399

St Francis of Assisi Church, 41. 42 Sciarappa St ☎ 876-6754

Sever Hall, 32. Harvard Yard

Stoughton House, 11. 90 Brattle St

Thomas Lee House, 6. 153 Brattle St

University Hall, 28. Harvard Yard

Wadsworth House, 27. Massachusetts Ave & Holyoke St

Widener Library, 30. Harvard Yard ☎ 495-2413

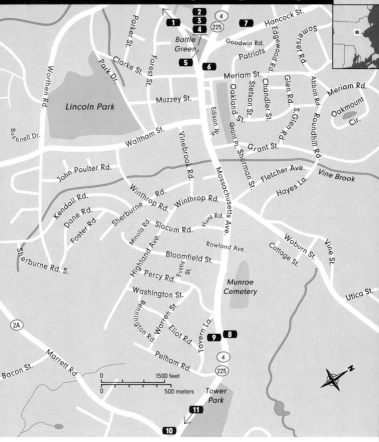

MAP 34 Exploring Salem

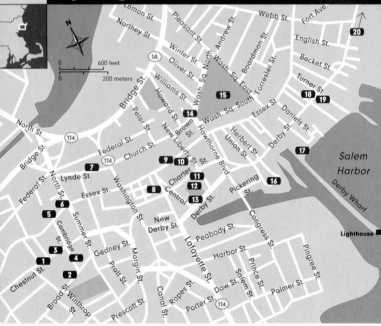

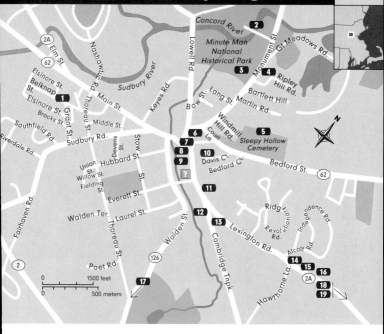

Exploring Concord

MAP 35

Listed by Site Number

1	Thoreau Lyceum	**7**	Monument Square	**13**	Concord Museum
2	Old North Bridge	**8**	Wright Tavern	**14**	Orchard House
3	Old Manse	**9**	First Parish Church	**15**	The Wayside Tavern
4	Bullet Hole House	**10**	Old Hill Burying Ground	**16**	Grapevine Cottage
5	Sleepy Hollow Cemetery	**11**	Hartwell Tavern	**17**	Thoreau's Cabin Site
6	Colonial Inn	**12**	Emerson House	**18**	Meriam's Corner
				19	Battle Rd Visitors Ctr

Listed Alphabetically

Battle Road Visitors Center, 19.
Rt 2A, Concord ☎ 617/862-7753

Bullet Hole House, 4.
Monument St, Concord

Colonial Inn, 6. 48 Monument Sq, Concord ☎ 508/369-9200

Concord Museum, 13.
200 Lexington Rd, Concord
☎ 508/369-9609

Emerson House, 12. 28 Cambridge Tnpk, Concord ☎ 508/369-2236

First Parish Church, 9. 20 Lexington Rd, Concord ☎ 508/369-9602

Grapevine Cottage, 16.
491 Lexington Rd, Concord

Hartwell Tavern, 11.
Lexington Rd, Concord

Meriam's Corner, 18.
Lexington Rd, Concord

Monument Square, 7. Concord

Old Hill Burying Ground, 10.
Lexington Rd, Concord

Old Manse, 3. Monument St, Concord ☎ 508/369-3909

Old North Bridge, 2.
174 Liberty St, Concord

Orchard House, 14. 399 Lexington Rd, Concord ☎ 508/369-4118

Sleepy Hollow Cemetery, 5.
Rt 62W, Concord

Thoreau's Cabin Site, 17.
Walden Pond, Rt 126, Concord

Thoreau Lyceum, 1. 156 Belknap St, Concord ☎ 508/369-5912

The Wayside Tavern, 15. 455 Lexington Rd, Concord ☎ 508/369-6975

Wright Tavern, 8. 2 Lexington Rd, Concord ☎ 508/369-9602

MAP 36 **Exploring Cape Ann**

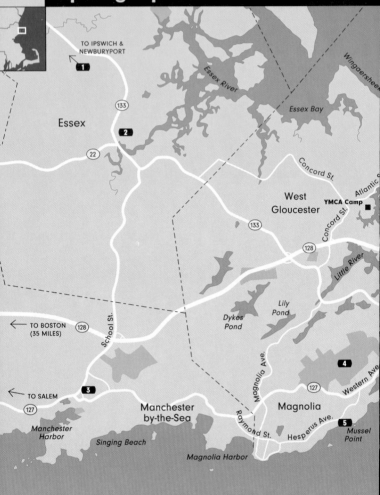

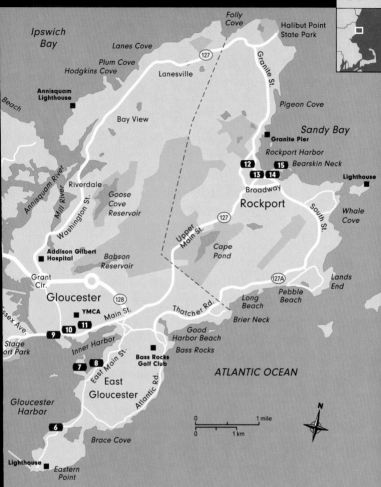

MAP 36

MAP 37 Parks & Recreation

ARLINGTON

Spy Pond

Broadway

Riverside Ave.

93

Mystic Ave.

16

Concord Tnpk.

2

2A

BELMONT

Columbus Memorial Park

Concord Ave.

Blanchard Rd.

Alewife Brook Pkwy.

Russell Field

Rindge Ave.

2A

Highland Ave.

Medford St.

Broadway

Foss Park

Fresh Pond Golf Course

Fresh Pond

Kingsley Park

Concord Ave.

Porter Sq.

Summer St.

SOMERVILLE

Somerville Ave.

Union Sq.

Washington St.

28

School St.

Arlington St.

Huron Ave.

Fresh Pond Pkwy.

Huron Ave.

Aberdeen Ave.

Brattle St.

Gorden St.

Oxford St.

Beacon St.

Belmont St.

Mt. Auburn St.

Harvard Sq.

Kirkland St.

Cambridge St.

Common St.

Oakley Country Club

16

Broadway

Prospect St.

Hampshire St.

WATERTOWN

Mt. Auburn St.

Grove St.

JFK St.

N. Harvard St.

Harvard St.

CAMBRIDGE

Central Sq.

Broadway

School St.

20

Arsenal St.

Dr. P. D. White Charles River Bike Path

Soldiers Field Rd.

Western Ave.

River St.

Magazine St.

Brookline St.

Massachusetts Ave.

Main St.

Memorial Dr.

Briggs Field (MIT)

90

20

ALLSTON

Dr. P. D. White Charles River Bike Path

2

3

90

Boston U. Bridge

Harvard Bridge

Storrow Dr.

Charles

N. Beacon St.

Market St.

Cambridge St.

Harvard Ave.

Brighton Ave.

Commonwealth Ave.

2

Commonwealth

Beacon St.

Washington St.

Ringer Park

BRIGHTON

Harvard St.

Beacon St.

Riverway

Back Bay Fens

Gallagher Memorial Park

Chandler Pond

Lake St.

Chestnut Hill Ave.

Commonwealth Ave.

Washington St.

Huntington Ave.

New Dudley St.

9

Commonwealth Ave.

Beacon St.

ROXBURY

Beacon St.

Chestnut Hill Res.

Chestnut Hill Park

Brookline Reservoir

Leverett Pond

Washington Park

Hammond's Pond

Hammond Pond Pkwy.

Boylston St.

BROOKLINE

Olmstead Park

Perkins St.

Centre St.

Columbus Ave.

9

28

Dane Park

Lee St.

Larz Anderson Park

Jamaica Pond

Centre St.

Washington St.

Brookline Golf Course

Newton St.

JAMAICA PLAIN

Franklin Park

Seaver St.

Brookline St.

William Devine Golf Course

28

The Boston Marathon

20 Watertown Cambridge Boston

Newton

Commonwealth Ave. Beacon St.

FINISH

Marlborough

90

16

9

Brookline

1

1

9 Framingham Wellesley

135 Natick

95 Dedham

28

Milton 93

START

495 Hopkinton

16

109

Morton St.

American Legion Hwy.

Franklin Field

Talbot Ave.

Blue Hill Ave.

Woodrow Ave.

MAP **37**

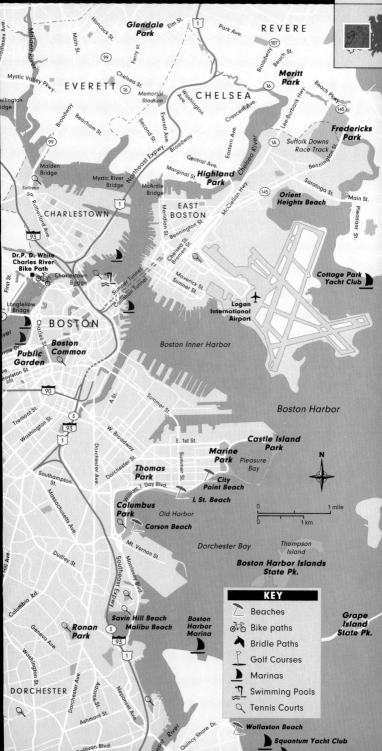

REVERE

Glendale
Park

Park Ave.

107

Meritt
Park

Broadway

Beach St.

Hancock St.

Elm St.

1

Main St.

Malden River

Middlesex Ave.

Mystic Valley Pkwy.

Ferry st.

99

EVERETT

16

Chelsea St.

Memorial
Stadium

CHELSEA

16

Beach Pkwy.

145

Lee-Burbank Hwy.

Fredericks
Park

Washington Ave.

Crescent Ave.

1A

Suffolk Downs
Race Track

Second St.

Everett Ave.

Broadway

Central Ave.

Eastern Ave.

Chelsea River

Bennington St.

Saratoga St.

Pleasant St.

Main St.

ellington
dge

Broadway

Beacham St.

99

Malden
Bridge

Mystic River
Bridge

Marginal St.

Highland
Park

McClellan Hwy.

145

Orient
Heights Beach

Sullivan
Sq.

McArdle
Bridge

Meridian St.

EAST
BOSTON

Bennington St.

CHARLESTOWN

Rutherford Ave.

1

93

First St.

Dr. P. D. White
Charles River
Bike Path

Charlestown
Bridge

Sumner Tunnel

Callahan Tunnel

Chelsea St.
Bremen St.

Maverick St.
Sumner St.

Logan
International
Airport

Cottage Park
Yacht Club

Longfellow
Bridge

BOSTON

Boston
Common

Charles St.

Public
Garden

arrow
Dr.

Boston Inner Harbor

Boston Harbor

Boylston St.

90

Tremont St.

Washington St.

3

93

1

A St.

W. Broadway

Summer St.

Dorchester St.

E. 1st St.

Marine
Park

Castle Island
Park

Pleasure
Bay

N

Southampton
St.

Dorchester Ave.

Thomas
Park

Summer St.

William J. Day Blvd.

City
Point Beach

L St. Beach

Massachusetts Ave.

Columbus
Park

Old Harbor

Carson Beach

Mt. Vernon St.

Dorchester Bay

Thompson
Island

Boston Harbor Islands
State Pk.

0   1 mile

0   1 km

Hill Ave.

Columbia Rd.

Dudley St.

Southeast Expwy.

Morrissey Blvd.

Ronan
Park

3

93

Savin Hill Beach
Malibu Beach

Boston
Harbor
Marina

Grape
Island
State Pk.

Geneva Ave.

Washington St.

Dorchester Ave.

Adams St.

Ashmont St.

DORCHESTER

Neponset Ave.

Quincy Shore Dr.

Wollaston Beach

Squantum Yacht Club

Gallivan Blvd.

KEY

Beaches

Bike paths

Bridle Paths

Golf Courses

Marinas

Swimming Pools

Tennis Courts

MAP 38 The Emerald Necklace

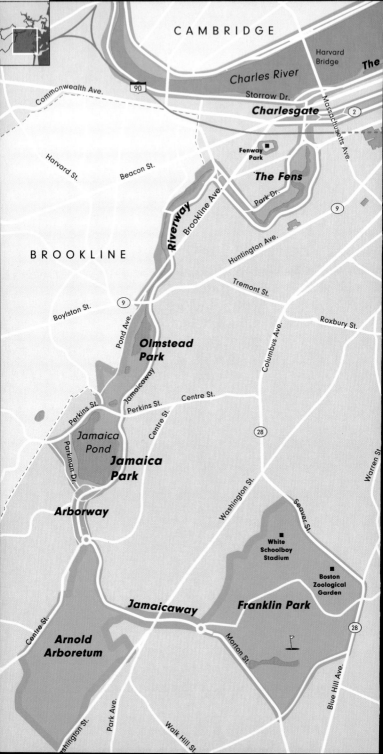

CAMBRIDGE

Harvard Bridge

Charles River

Storrow Dr.

Commonwealth Ave.

90

Charlesgate

2

Harvard St.

Beacon St.

Fenway Park

The Fens

Park Dr.

9

Riverway

Brookline Ave.

Huntington Ave.

B R O O K L I N E

Tremont St.

Boylston St.

9

Roxbury St.

Pond Ave.

Olmstead Park

Columbus Ave.

Jamaicaway

Perkins St.

Perkins St.

Centre St.

Centre St.

28

Jamaica Pond

Parkman Dr.

Jamaica Park

Centre St.

Washington St.

Warren St.

Arborway

White Schoolboy Stadium

Seaver St.

Jamaicaway

Franklin Park

Boston Zoological Garden

28

Arnold Arboretum

Centre St.

Morton St.

Blue Hill Ave.

Washington St.

Park Ave.

Walk Hill St.

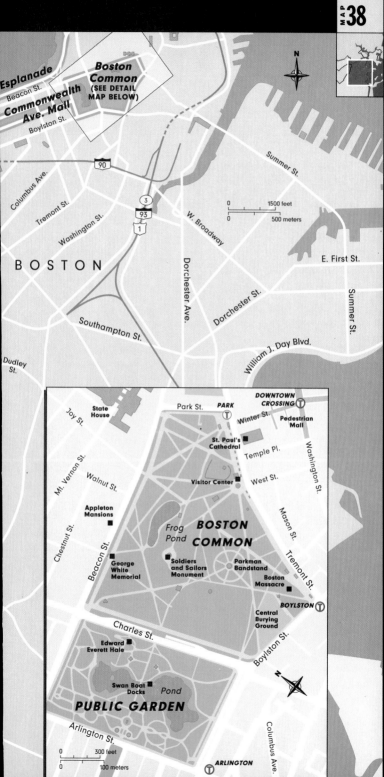

MAP 38

Esplanade

Beacon St.

Commonwealth
Ave. Mall

Boylston St.

Boston
Common
(SEE DETAIL
MAP BELOW)

N

90

3

93

1

Columbus Ave.

Tremont St.

Washington St.

BOSTON

Summer St.

W. Broadway

Dorchester St.

E. First St.

Southampton St.

Dorchester Ave.

Dorchester St.

Summer St.

Dudley
St.

William J. Day Blvd.

0   1500 feet
0   500 meters

Joy St.

State
House

Park St.

PARK

DOWNTOWN
CROSSING

Winter St.

Pedestrian
Mall

Mt. Vernon St.

Walnut St.

St. Paul's
Cathedral

Temple Pl.

Washington St.

Appleton
Mansions

Visitor Center

West St.

Chestnut St.

Beacon St.

Frog
Pond

BOSTON
COMMON

Mason St.

Tremont St.

George
White
Memorial

Soldiers
and Sailors
Monument

Parkman
Bandstand

Boston
Massacre

BOYLSTON

Central
Burying
Ground

Charles St.

Boylston St.

Edward
Everett Hale

Swan Boat
Docks

Pond

PUBLIC GARDEN

Arlington St.

Columbus Ave.

N

0   300 feet
0   100 meters

ARLINGTON

MAP 39 Beaches

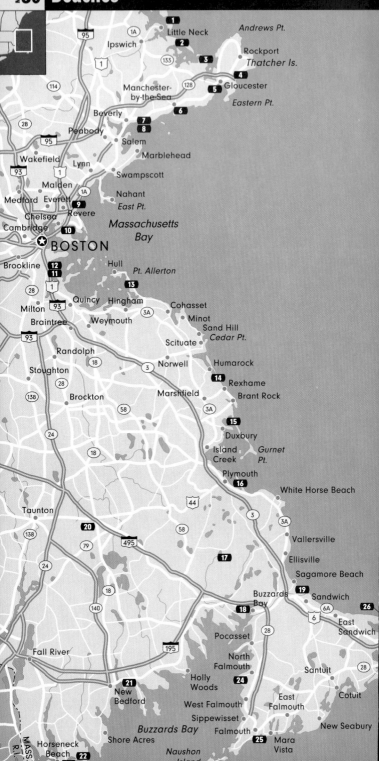

MAP 39

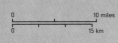

ATLANTIC OCEAN

Race Pt.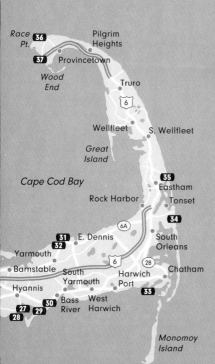

Pilgrim Heights

Provincetown

Wood End

Truro

6

Wellfleet   S. Wellfleet

Great Island

Cape Cod Bay

Rock Harbor

35
Eastham
Tonset

34

6A

31   E. Dennis
32

Yarmouth

Barnstable   South
Yarmouth

Hyannis

27   30   Bass   West
29   River   Harwich
28

South
Orleans

28

Harwich
Port

33

Chatham

Monomoy
Island

Nantucket Sound

0   10 miles
0   15 km

N

MAP 39 Beaches

Listed Alphabetically

NORTH SHORE

Crane's Beach, 2. Ipswich
☎ 508/356-4354. *R,L,F,P*

Cressy Beach, 5.
Stage Fort Pk, Gloucester. *R*

Dane St, 7. Beverly
☎ 508/922-9582. *R,L,P*

Good Harbor, 4. Thatcher Rd,
Gloucester ☎ 508/281-0381. *R,L,F,P*

Lynch Park, 8. Ober St, Beverly
☎ 508/921-6067. *L,P*

Plum Island, 1. Newburyport
☎ 508/462-6680. *R,L*

Singing Beach, 6. Manchester. *R,L*

Wingaersheek, 3. Concord St,
Gloucester ☎ 508/281-4835. *R,L,F,P*

GREATER BOSTON

Constitution Beach, 10. E Boston
☎ 567-9272 *R,L,F,P*

Malibu Beach, 11. Dorchester
☎ 288-2088. *R,L,F,P*

Revere Beach, 9. Rt IA,
Revere Beach ☎ 284-5121. *R,L,F,P*

Savin Hill Beach, 12.
Dorchester. *R,L,F,P*

SOUTH SHORE

College/Fearing Ponds, 17.
Plymouth ☎ 508/866-2526. *R,P*

Duxbury Beach, 15. Duxbury
☎ 934-6586. *R,L,F,P*

Humarock Beach, 14. Marshfield
☎ 545-8740. *R,L*

Nantasket Beach, 13. Hull
☎ 925-2000. *R,L,F,P*

Onset Beach, 18. Wareham
☎ 508/291-3101. *F,P*

Plymouth Beach, 16. Plymouth
☎ 508/830-4095. *L,F,P*

Scusset Beach, 19. Bourne
☎ 508/888-0859. *R,F,P*

BRISTOL COUNTY

Demarest Lloyd State Park, 22.
Dartmouth ☎ 508/636-3298. *R,L*

Fort Phoenix State Park, 21.
Fairhaven ☎ 508/992-4524. *R,L*

Horseneck Beach, 23. Westport
☎ 508/636-8816. *R,L*

Massasoit State Park, 20. E Taunton
☎ 508/822-7405. *R,L*

CAPE COD

Bass River Beach, 30. So Shore Dr,
Bass River ☎ 508/398-2231. *R,F,P*

Coast Guard Beach, 35.
Rt 6, Eastham ☎ 508/255-0338. *R,F,P*

Corporation Rd Beach, 31.
Rt 6A, Dennis ☎ 508/394-8300. *R,F,P*

Harding's Beach, 33. Rt 28,
W Chatham ☎ 508/945-5158. *R,F*

Herring Cove, 37. Rt 6, Provincetown
☎ 508/487-7097. *R,F,P*

Kalmus Park, 27. Ocean St, Hyannis
☎ 508/790-6345. *R,F,P*

Orrin Keyes, 28. Sea St, Hyannis
☎ 508/790-6345. *R,F,P*

Mayflower Beach, 32. Rt 6A, Dennis
☎ 508/394-8300. *R,F,P*

Nauset Beach, 34. Rt 28, E Orleans
☎ 508/240-3785. *R,F,P*

Old Silver, 24. Quaker Rd,
No Falmouth ☎ 508/457-2567. *R,F,P*

Race Point, 36. Rt 6, Provincetown
☎ 508/487-7097. *R*

Sandy Neck, 26. Rt 6A, W Barnstable
☎ 508/790-6345. *R,F,P*

Sea Gull, 29. South Sea Ave,
W Yarmouth ☎ 508/398-2231. *R,F,P*

Surf Drive, 25. Surf Dr, Falmouth
☎ 508/457-2567. *R,F,P*

R=Restrooms L=Lifeguard F=Food P=Parking

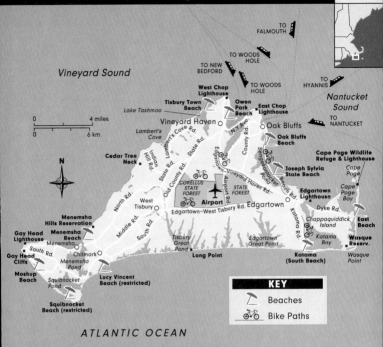

Martha's Vineyard

Vineyard Sound

TO FALMOUTH

TO WOODS HOLE

TO NEW BEDFORD

TO WOODS HOLE

TO HYANNIS

Nantucket Sound

TO NANTUCKET

West Chop Lighthouse

Tisbury Town Beach

Owen Park Beach

East Chop Lighthouse

Lake Tashmoo

Vineyard Haven

Oak Bluffs

Oak Bluffs Beach

Lambert's Cove

Cape Poge Wildlife Refuge & Lighthouse

Cedar Tree Neck

Joseph Sylvia State Beach

Cape Poge

Cape Poge Bay

West Tisbury

Airport

Edgartown Lighthouse

Dyke Rd.

Chappaquiddick Island

East Beach

Edgartown

Edgartown-West Tisbury Rd.

Katama Bay

Wasque Reserv.

Menemsha Hills Reservation

Menemsha Beach

Menemsha

Tisbury Great Pond

Edgartown Great Pond

Katama (South Beach)

Wasque Point

Gay Head Lighthouse

Chilmark

Menemsha Pond

Long Point

Gay Head Cliffs

Moshup Beach

Squibnocket Pond

Lucy Vincent Beach (restricted)

Squibnocket Beach (restricted)

ATLANTIC OCEAN

KEY

Beaches

Bike Paths

0 4 miles
0 6 km

N

CORELLUS STATE FOREST

Vineyard Haven Rd.

STATE FOREST

Cedar Tree Neck

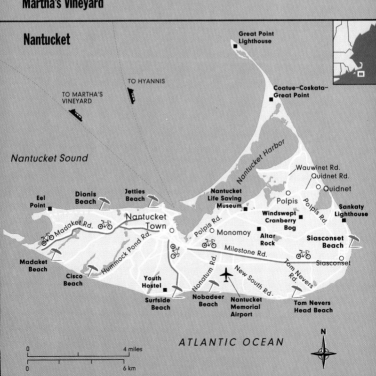

Nantucket

Great Point Lighthouse

TO HYANNIS

Coatue-Coskata-Great Point

TO MARTHA'S VINEYARD

Nantucket Sound

Nantucket Harbor

Wauwinet Rd.
Quidnet Rd.

Quidnet

Eel Point

Dionis Beach

Jetties Beach

Nantucket Life Saving Museum

Polpis

Polpis Rd.

Sankaty Lighthouse

Nantucket Town

Madaket Rd.

Windswept Cranberry Bog

Polpis Rd.

Monomoy

Altar Rock

Siasconset Beach

Madaket Beach

Hummock Pond Rd.

Milestone Rd.

Siasconset

Cisco Beach

Youth Hostel

Nonatum Rd.

New South Rd.

Tom Nevers Rd.

Surfside Beach

Nobadeer Beach

Nantucket Memorial Airport

Tom Nevers Head Beach

ATLANTIC OCEAN

0 4 miles
0 6 km

N

MAP 41 Stadiums & Arenas/Foxboro Stadium

Foxboro Access

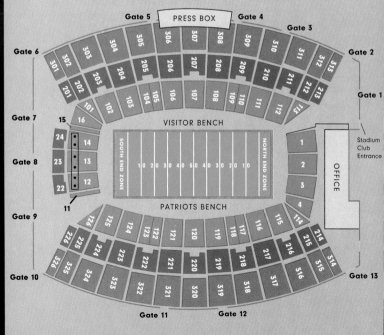

Foxboro Stadium

Boston Garden

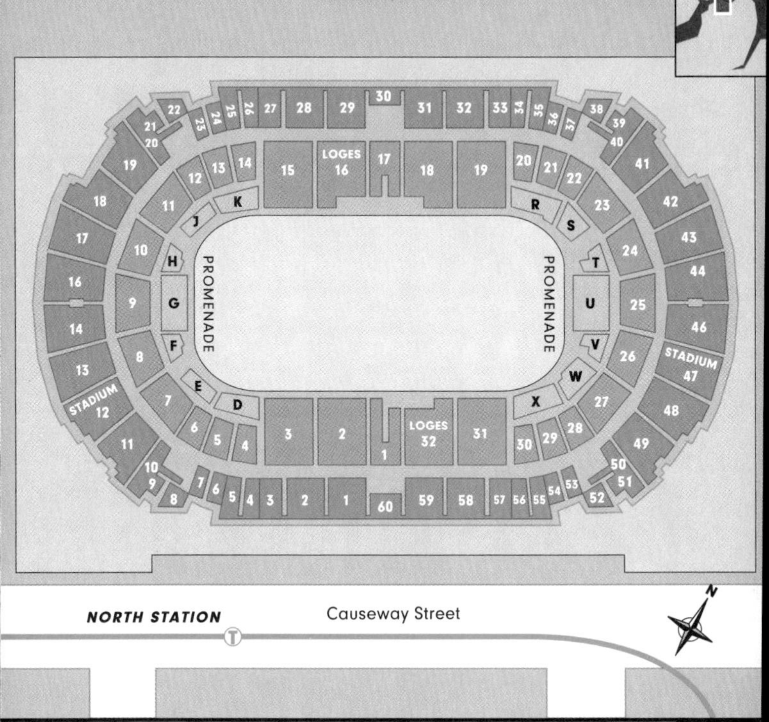

26
21 22 23 24 25 27 28 29 30 31 32 33 34 35 36 37 38 39
20 40
19 LOGES 20
12 13 14 15 16 17 18 19 21
18 11 K 22 42
J R
17 10 H S 23 43
16 G T 24 44
H
14 9 G PROMENADE PROMENADE U 25 46
13 8 F V 26 STADIUM 47
STADIUM 12 7 E D W 27 48
11 6 5 4 X 28 49
10 3 2 LOGES 31 30 29 50
9 1 32 51
8 7 6 5 4 3 2 1 60 59 58 57 56 55 54 53 52

NORTH STATION   Causeway Street

T

N

Fenway Park

Brookline Ave.

Lansdowne Street

Gate E

Gate C

33
34 35 36 37 38
32
31 39
30 40
Gate A 29 41 Bleachers
28 42
ROOF BOX SEATS 27 43
26 1
25 2
24 3
23 Gate B
22 4
Yawkey Way 21 5
20 Field Box Seats 6 7
19 Box Seats 8 9 10 11
18 17 16 15 14 13 12 Grandstand/Reserved
Roof Box Seats

Gate D   Van Ness Street

Parking

N

Parking

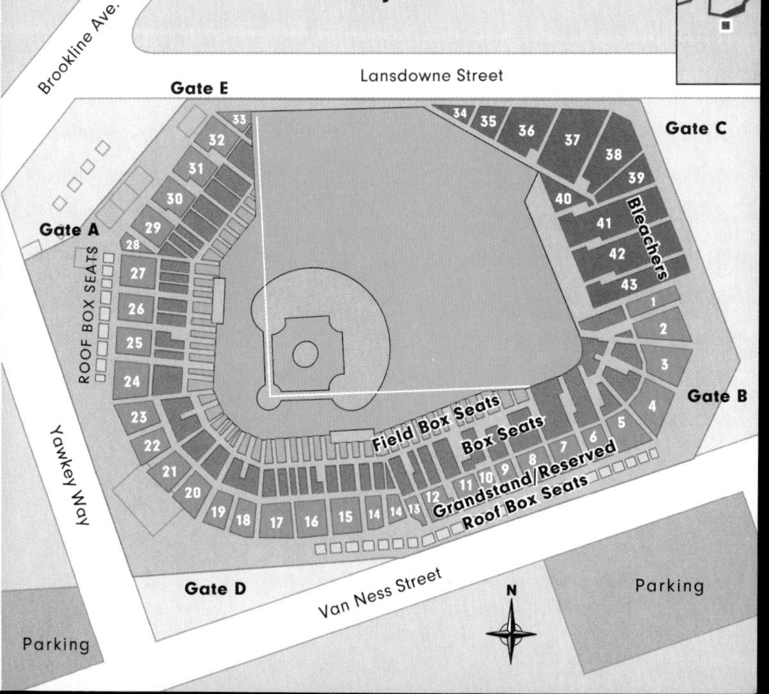

MAP 42 **Shopping/Back Bay**

Listed by Site Number

1   Boston University Bookstore Mall
2   EMS
3   Tower Records
4   Selletto
5   Safar X-S-R-E
6   Saks Fifth Ave
7   Lord & Taylor
8   Emporio Armani
9   Next
10 Kitchen Arts
11 Bally
11 Disney Store
11 Tiffany & Co
11 Victoria's Secret
12 A/X Armani Exchange
12 Godiva Chocolatier
13 Jaeger
14 Neiman Marcus
15 The Sharper Image
15 Joan & David
16 Gucci
16 Louis Vuitton
16 Rizzoli Book Store
17 Barnes & Noble
18 Rodier
19 Lou Lou's Lost & Found
20 Fogai

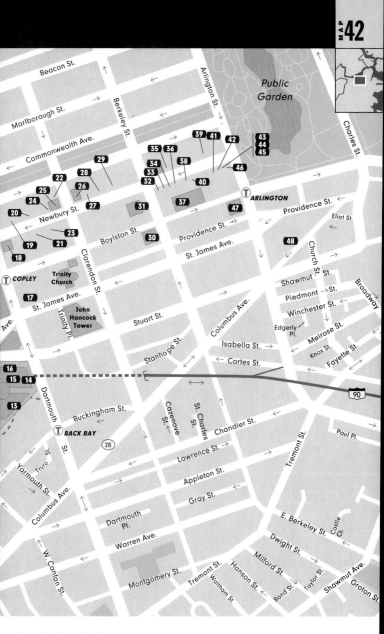

MAP **42**

Beacon St.

Marlborough St.

Berkeley St.

Arlington St.

Marlborough St.

Commonwealth Ave.

Public
Garden

Charles St.

39 **41** **42**

43
44
45

35 **36**

34

33

32

38

29

28

22

25

26

24

27

20

Newbury St.

31

40

46

Ⓣ ARLINGTON

Providence St.

Eliot St.

23

21

19

18

Boylston St.

30

37

47

Providence St.

St. James Ave.

48

Church St.

St.

Broadway

Ⓣ COPLEY

Trinity
Church

Shawmut St.

Piedmont St.

Winchester St.

Melrose St.

17

St. James Ave.

John
Hancock
Tower

Stuart St.

Columbus Ave.

Edgerly
Pl.

Knox St.

Fayette St.

Trinity Pl.

Ave.

16

15 **14**

13

Dartmouth St.

Buckingham St.

Ⓣ BACK BAY

(28)

Stanhope St.

Cazenove
St.

St. Charles
St.

Isabella St.

Cortes St.

Chandler St.

90

Paul Pl.

Yarmouth St.

Truro
St.

Columbus Ave.

Lawrence St.

Appleton St.

Gray St.

Tremont St.

W. Canton St.

Dartmouth
Pl.

Warren Ave.

E. Berkeley St.

Castle
Ct.

Dwight St.

Milford St.

Montgomery St.

Tremont St.

Waltham St.

Hanson St.

Bond St.

Taylor St.

Shawmut Ave.

Groton St.

MAP 42 **Shopping/Back Bay**

Listed Alphabetically

Alan Bilzerian, 36.
34 Newbury St ☎ 536-1001

Allen Edmonds, 34.
36 Newbury St ☎ 247-3363

Ann Taylor, 41. 18 Newbury St
☎ 262-0763

A/X Armani Exchange, 12.
Copley Place ☎ 262-4300

Bally, 11. Copley Place ☎ 437-1910

Barnes & Noble, 17. Copley Square
☎ 236-1308

**Boston University Bookstore
Mall, 1.** 660 Beacon St ☎ 267-8484

Brooks Brothers, 32. 46 Newbury St
☎ 267-2600

Burberrys Ltd, 46. 2 Newbury St
☎ 236-1000

Cartier, 33. 40 Newbury St ☎ 262-3300

Charles Sumner, 42. 16 Newbury St
☎ 536-6225

Cole Haan, 25. 109 Newbury St
☎ 536-7826

Disney Store, 11. Copley Place
☎ 266-5200

Domain, 39. 7 Newbury St
☎ 266-5252

Dorfman, 38. 24 Newbury St
☎ 536-2022

EMS, 2. 1041 Commonwealth Ave
☎ 254-4250

Emporio Armani, 8. 210 Newbury St
☎ 262-7300

FAO Schwarz, 30. 440 Boylston St
☎ 266-5101

Fogal, 20. 115 Newbury St ☎ 262-5338

Giorgio Armani, 40. 22 Newbury St
☎ 267-3200

Godiva Chocolatier, 12.
Copley Place ☎ 437-8490

Gucci, 16. Copley Place ☎ 247-3000

Jaeger, 13. 4 Copley Place ☎ 437-1163

Joan & David, 15. 2 Copley Place
☎ 536-0600

JoS A Bank, 21. 122 Newbury St
☎ 536-5050

Joseph Abboud, 35. 37 Newbury St
☎ 266-4200

Kakas, 27. 93 Newbury St ☎ 536-1858

Kitchen Arts, 10. 161 Newbury St
☎ 266-8701

L J Peretti & Co, 48. Park Square
☎ 482-0218

Laura Ashley, 28. 83 Newbury St
☎ 536-0505

Lewis John, 26. 97 Newbury St
☎ 266-6665

Lord & Taylor, 7. 760 Boylston St
☎ 262-6000

Lou Lou's Lost & Found, 19.
121 Newbury St ☎ 859-8593

Louis Vuitton, 16. Copley Place
☎ 437-6519

Louis Boston, 31. 234 Berkeley St
☎ 262-6100

Martini Carl, 29. 77 Newbury St
☎ 247-0441

MCM, 45. 4 Newbury St ☎ 262-7276

Neiman Marcus, 14. 5 Copley Place
☎ 536-3660

Next, 9. 208 Newbury St ☎ 236-6398

OKW, 22. 234 Clarendon St ☎ 266-4114

Pierre Deux, 24. 111 Newbury St
☎ 536-6364

Pratesi, 23. 110 Newbury St ☎ 262-5998

Rizzoli Book Store, 16. Copley Place
☎ 437-0700

Rodier, 18. 144 Newbury St
☎ 247-2410

Roots, 37. 419 Boylston St ☎ 247-0700

Safar X-S-R-E, 5. 233 Newbury St
☎ 353-0942

Saks Fifth Ave, 6. Prudential Center
☎ 262-8500

Selletto, 4. 244 Newbury St
☎ 424-0656

Shreve, Crump & Low, 47.
330 Boylston St ☎ 267-9100

Stuarts Inc, 43. 10 Newbury St
☎ 267-6900

The Sharper Image, 15.
Copley Place ☎ 262-7010

Tiffany & Co, 11. Copley Place
☎ 353-0222

Tower Records, 3. 360 Newbury St
☎ 247-5900

Verona, 44. 8A Newbury St
☎ 536-2425

Victoria's Secret, 11. Copley Place
☎ 266-7505

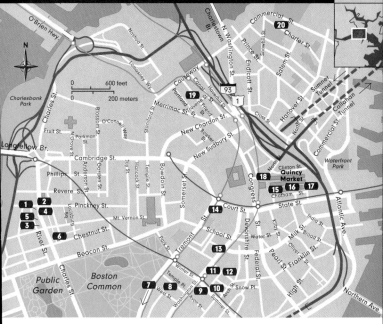

Listed by Site Number

1	Helen's Leather Shop	8	Brattle Bookstore	15	Coach
2	Boston Antiques Coop	9	Jordan Marsh	16	Crate & Barrel
3	Jms Billings Antiques	10	Long's Jewelers	17	Brookstone
4	The Designers	11	Filene's	18	Signature
5	Matz & Pribell	12	London Harness Co	19	Hilton's Tent City
6	Kennedy Studio	13	Di Prisco	20	D'hajj
7	Freedburg of Boston	14	Eric Fuchs		

Listed Alphabetically

Boston Antiques Coop, 2.
119 Charles St ☎ 227-9810

Brattle Bookstore, 8. 9 West St
☎ 542-0210

Brookstone, 17. Faneuil Hall
Marketplace ☎ 439-4460

Coach, 15. Faneuil Hall Marketplace
☎ 723-1777

Crate & Barrel, 16. Faneuil Hall
Marketplace ☎ 742-6025

The Designers, 4. 103 Charles St
☎ 720-3967

D'hajj, 20. 502 Commercial St
☎ 367-1287

Di Prisco, 13. 333 Washington St
☎ 227-3339

Eric Fuchs, 14. 28 Tremont St
☎ 227-7935

Filene's, 11. 426 Washington St
☎ 357-2100

Freedburg of Boston, 7.
112 Shawmut Ave ☎ 357-8600

Helen's Leather Shop, 1.
110 Charles St ☎ 742-2077

Hilton's Tent City, 19. 272 Friend St
☎ 227-9242

James Billings Antiques, 3.
34 Charles St ☎ 367-9533

Jordan Marsh, 9.
450 Washington St ☎ 357-3000

Kennedy Studio, 6. 31 Charles St
☎ 523-9868

London Harness Co, 12.
60 Franklin St ☎ 542-9234

Long's Jewelers, 10. 40 Summer St
☎ 426-8500

Matz & Pribell, 5. 70 Charles St
☎ 227-3366

Signature, 18. Dock Square
☎ 227-4885

MAP 44 Shopping/Cambridge

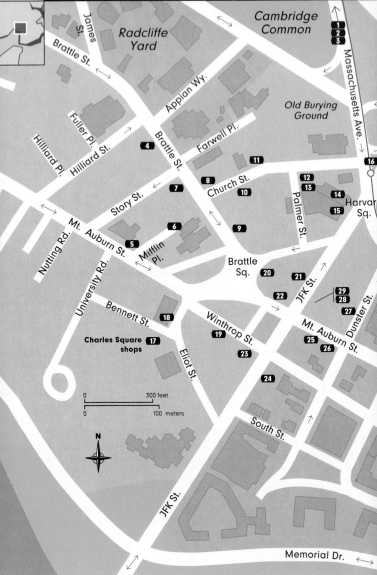

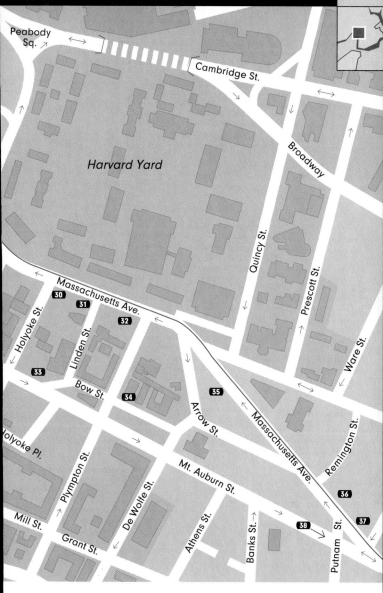

MAP 44 **Shopping/Cambridge**

Listed Alphabetically

Alpha Omega Jewelers, 23. 57 JFK St ☎ 864-1227

Banana Republic, 17. Charles Sq ☎ 497-8000

Barillari Books, 5. 1 Mifflin Place ☎ 864-2400

Bizarre Clothing, 29. 36 JFK St ☎ 876-2248

Blacksmith House Bakery, 4. 56 Brattle St ☎ 354-3036

Bob Slate, 1. 1975 Mass Ave ☎ 547-8624

The Body Shop, 14. 1440 Mass Ave ☎ 876-6334

The Bookcase, 10. 42 Church St ☎ 876-0832

Bowl & Board, 37. 1063 Mass Ave ☎ 661-0350

Briggs & Briggs, 32. 1270 Mass Ave ☎ 547-2007

Cambridge Artists' Coop, 11. 59A Church St ☎ 868-4434

Cheapo Records, 38. 645 Mass Ave ☎ 354-4455

Crabtree & Evelyn, 17. Charles Sq ☎ 576-6871

Crate & Barrel, 7. 48 Brattle St ☎ 876-6300

Dance Plus, 28. 34 JFK St ☎ 547-0263

Games People Play, 36. 1105 Mass Ave ☎ 492-0711

Globe Corner Bookstore, 12. 49 Palmer St ☎ 497-6277

Good Good the Elephant, 19. 106 Winthrop St ☎ 547-9691

Grolier Bookshop, 34. 6 Plympton St ☎ 547-4648

HMV USA, 6. 1 Brattle Sq ☎ 868-9696

Harvard Coop, 15. 1400 Mass Ave ☎ 499-2000

Harvard Shop, 24. 52 JFK St ☎ 576-3818

Herrell's, 27. 15 Dunster St ☎ 497-2179

Irish Imports, 2. 1735 Mass Ave ☎ 354-2511

J August, 30. 1320 Mass Ave ☎ 864-6650

Jasmine, 9. 37 Brattle St ☎ 354-6043

J Press, 26. 82 Mt Auburn St ☎ 547-9886

Laura Ashley, 17. Charles Sq ☎ 576-3690

Le Pli, 17. Charles Sq ☎ 868-8087

Leavitt & Peirce, 31. 1316 Mass Ave ☎ 547-0576

Limited Express, 6. 1 Brattle Square ☎ 547-9370

Newbury Comics, 29. 36 JFK St ☎ 491-0337

Out-of-Town News, 16. Harvard Sq ☎ 354-7777

Pangloss Bookshop, 33. 65 Mt Auburn St ☎ 354-4003

Papermint, 17. Charles Sq ☎ 492-0289

Passim Gallery, 13. 47 Palmer St ☎ 492-7679

Pepperweed, 3. 1684 Mass Ave ☎ 547-7561

Reading International, 8. 47 Brattle St ☎ 864-0705

Schoenhof's Foreign Books, 25. 76A Mt Auburn St ☎ 547-8855

Serendipity, 35. 1312 Mass Ave ☎ 661-7143

Taang! Records, 18. 12 Eliot St ☎ 876-2411

Talbot's, 17. Charles Sq ☎ 576-2278

Tower Records, 22. 95 Mt Auburn St ☎ 876-3377

Urban Outfitters, 21. 11 JFK St ☎ 864-0070

Vilunya, 17. Charles Sq ☎ 661-5753

W H Smith, 17. Charles Sq ☎ 492-6898

Wordsworth, 20. 30 Brattle St ☎ 354-5201

Shopping Centers/Boston Area

MAP 45

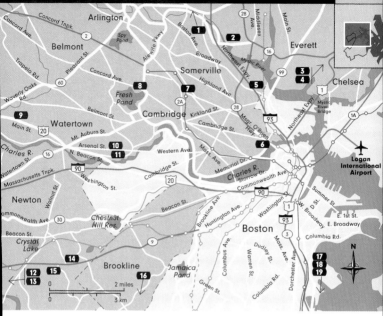

Listed by Site Number

1 Burlington Mall
2 Meadow Glen Mall
3 Liberty Tree Mall
4 Northshore Mall
5 Assembly Square Mall
6 Cambridgeside Galleria

7 Porter Square Arcade
8 Fresh Pond Mall
9 Colonial Mall
10 Watertown Mall
11 Arsenal Mall
12 Natick Mall

13 Shoppers' World
14 Chestnut Hill Mall
15 Atrium Mall
16 Walpole Mall
17 Emerald Sq Mall
18 Harbor Light Mall
19 South Shore Plaza

Listed Alphabetically

Arsenal Mall, 11. 485 Arsenal St, Watertown ☎ 923-4700

Assembly Square Mall, 5. 133 Middlesex Ave, Somerville ☎ 628-3800

Atrium Mall, 15. 300 Boylston St, Chestnut Hill ☎ 527-1400

Burlington Mall, 1. Rt 128, Burlington ☎ 272-8667

Cambridgeside Galleria, 6. 100 Cambridgeside Place, Cambridge ☎ 621-8666

Chestnut Hill Mall, 14. 199 Boylston St, Newton ☎ 965-3037

Colonial Mall, 9. 85 River St, Waltham ☎ 899-3749

Emerald Square Mall, 17. Rt 1, No Attleboro ☎ 508/699-7979

Fresh Pond Mall, 8. 186 Alewife Pkwy, Cambridge ☎ 491-4431

Harbor Light Mall, 18. 789 Bridge St, Weymouth ☎ 335-3395

Liberty Tree Mall, 3. Rt 128, Danvers ☎ 508/777-0794

Meadow Glen Mall, 2. 3850 Mystic Valley Pkwy, Medford ☎ 395-1010

Natick Mall, 12. 1345 Worcester St, Natick ☎ 237-0217

Northshore Mall, 4. Rts 128 & 114, Peabody ☎ 508/531-3440

Porter Square Arcade, 7. 1 Porter Sq, Cambridge ☎ 576-2939

Shoppers' World, 13. Rts 9 & 30, Framingham ☎ 508/872-1256

South Shore Plaza, 19. 250 Granite St, Braintree ☎ 843-8200

Walpole Mall, 16. 90 Providence Hwy, Walpole ☎ 769-9040

Watertown Mall, 10. 550 Arsenal St, Watertown ☎ 926-4123

MAP 46 Restaurants/Downtown

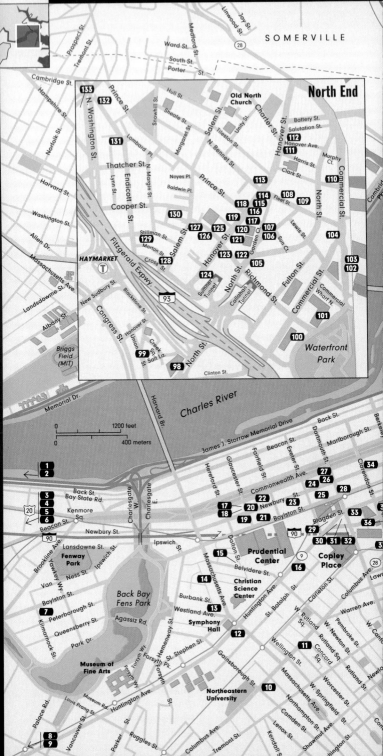

SOMERVILLE

North End

Old North Church

HAYMARKET

Charles River

James J. Storrow Memorial Drive

Briggs Field (MIT)

Memorial Dr.

Waterfront Park

0   1200 feet
0   400 meters

Kenmore Sq.

Fenway Park

Back Bay Fens Park

Prudential Center

Christian Science Center

Copley Place

Symphony Hall

Museum of Fine Arts

Northeastern University

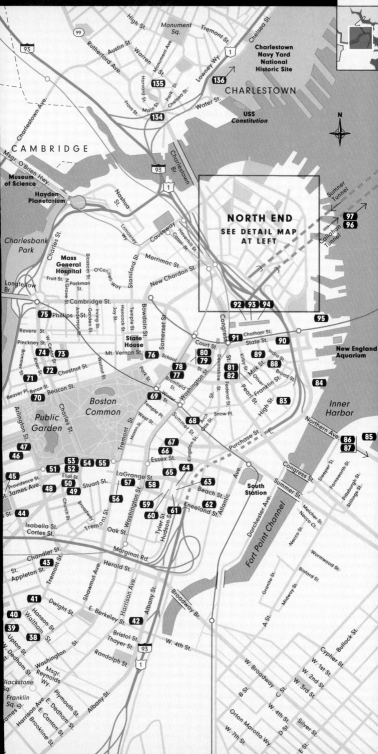

MAP 46 **Restaurants/Downtown**

Listed by Site Number

1 Sports Depot
2 Scullers Grille
3 Enzo's
4 Village Fish
5 Veronique
6 Sol Azteca
7 Stars Ocean
8 The Blue Nile
9 Sawasdee
10 Bob the Chef
11 Jae's Cafe
12 Selaam
13 Thai Cuisine
14 Bangkok Cuisine
15 Boodles of Boston
16 Bello Mondo
17 L'Espalier
18 Casa Romero
19 Charley's Eating and Drinking Saloon
20 Miyako
21 Gyuhama
22 Davio's
23 Emporio Armani Express
24 TGI Friday's
25 Mr. Leung
26 Du Barry
27 Spasso
28 Papa Razzi
29 Cafe Budapest
30 Ten Huntington
31 House of Siam
32 Turner Fisheries
33 Plaza Dining Room
34 Mirabelle
35 Skipjack's
36 Hard Rock Cafe
37 Bertucci's
38 On the Park
39 Hamersley's Bistro
40 Botolph's on Tremont
41 St Cloud
42 Medieval Manor Theatre Restaurant
43 Icarus
44 Grill 23
45 Cottonwood Cafe
46 29 Newbury
47 Ritz Cafe
48 Legal Sea Foods

49 Kyoto
50 Star of Siam
51 Biba
52 Aujourd'hui
53 Bristol Lounge
54 Rocco's
55 Marais
56 Montien
57 Jacob Wirth
58 Pho Pasteur
59 Siam Square
60 Carl's Pagoda
61 Golden Palace
62 Blue Diner
63 Ho Yuen Ting
64 Asian Garden Seafood Restaurant
65 Chau Chow
66 Morton's of Chicago
67 Café Suisse
68 Dakota's
69 Locke-Ober Cafe
70 Library Grill at Hampshire House
71 Charles Restaurant
72 Ristorante Toscano
73 Another Season
74 Hungry I
75 King & I
76 Black Goose
77 Cafe Marliave
78 Parker's
79 Ben's Cafe
80 Maison Robert
81 Cafe Fleuri
82 Julien
83 Nara
84 Rowes Wharf Restaurant
85 No Name
86 Anthonys Pier 4
87 Jimmy's Harborside
88 Sakura-bana
89 Schifino
90 Tatsukichi
91 Bay Tower Room
92 Brasserie Les Halles
93 Durgin Park
94 Zumas Tex-Mex Cafe
95 Chart House
96 Sablone's

97 Domenico's
98 Seasons
99 Union Oyster House
100 Joseph's Aquarium
101 Cornucopia on the Wharf
102 Michael's Waterfront
103 Boston Sail Loft
104 Jasper's
105 Florence's
106 Mamma Maria
107 Five North Square
108 Bernardo's
109 La Summa
110 Davide
111 Ristorante Lucia
112 Bella Napoli
113 Cantina Italiana
114 Emilio's
115 Giacomo's
116 Mateo's
117 G'Vanni's
118 Carlo Marino
119 Caffe Vittoria
120 Daily Catch
121 Galeria Umberto
122 Felicia's
123 Villa Francesca
124 Mother Anna's
125 Saraceno's
126 Il Panino
127 L'Osteria
128 Nicole
129 Pushcart
130 Dom's
131 Oasis Cafe
132 Massimino's
133 Filippo
134 Olives
135 Figs
136 Rita's Place

MAP 46

Listed Alphabetically

Another Season, 73.
97 Mt Vernon St
☎ 367-0880. French/American. $$$$

Anthonys Pier 4, 86.
140 Northern Ave
☎ 423-6363. Seafood. $$$$

**Asian Garden Seafood
Restaurant, 64.** 46 Beach St
☎ 695-1646. Chinese. $

Aujourd'hui, 52.
Four Seasons Hotel, 200 Boylston St
☎ 451-1392. Continental. $$$$

Bangkok Cuisine, 14. 177A Mass Ave
☎ 262-5377. Thai. $$

Bay Tower Room, 91. 60 State St
☎ 723-1666. American. $$$$

Bella Napoli, 112. 425 Hanover St
☎ 720-2811. Italian. $$

Bello Mondo, 16.
Marriott Copley Place
☎ 236-5800. Italian. $$$

Ben's Cafe, 79. 45 School St
☎ 227-3370. Traditional. $$$

Bernardo's, 108. 24 Fleet St
☎ 723-4554. Italian. $$

Bertucci's, 37. 39 Stanhope St
☎ 247-6161. Pizza. $

Biba, 51. 272 Boylston St
☎ 426-7878. Eclectic. $$$$

Black Goose, 76. 21 Beacon St
☎ 720-4500. Italian. $$

Blue Diner, 62. 178 Kneeland St
☎ 338-4639. American. $

The Blue Nile, 8. 23 S Huntington Ave
☎ 731-3833. Ethiopian. $

Bob the Chef, 10. 604 Columbus Ave
☎ 536-6204. Soul food. $

Boodles of Boston, 15.
Back Bay Hilton
☎ 266-3537. Steak. $$$

Boston Sail Loft, 103. 80 Atlantic Ave
☎ 227-7250. Seafood. $$

Botolph's on Tremont, 40.
569 Tremont St
☎ 424-8577. Italian/American. $$

Brasserie Les Halles, 92.
301 Faneuil Hall Marketplace
☎ 227-1272. French. $$$

Bristol Lounge, 53.
Four Seasons Hotel, 200 Boylston St
☎ 338-4400. American. $$$

Cafe Budapest, 29.
Copley Hotel, 90 Exeter St
☎ 266-1979. Continental. $$$$

Cafe Fleuri, 81. Hotel Meridien,
20 Franklin St ☎ 451-1900. French. $$$

Cafe Marliave, 77. 10 Bosworth St
☎ 423-6340. Italian. $$

Café Suisse, 67. Swissôtel,
1 Ave de Lafayette
☎ 451-2600. Continental. $$$

Caffe Vittoria, 119. 294 Hanover St
☎ 227-7606. Italian. $

Cantina Italiana, 113. 346 Hanover St
☎ 723-4577. Italian. $$

Carlo Marino, 118. 8 Prince St
☎ 523-9109. Italian. $$

Carl's Pagoda, 60. 23 Tyler St
☎ 357-9837. Chinese. $$

Casa Romero, 18. 30 Gloucester St
☎ 536-4341. Mexican. $$

Charles Restaurant, 71. 75 Chestnut St
☎ 523-4477. Italian. $$$

**Charley's Eating and Drinking
Saloon, 19.** 284 Newbury St
☎ 266-3000. American. $$

Chart House, 95. 60 Long Wharf
☎ 227-1576. Seafood. $$$

Chau Chow, 65. 52 Beach St
☎ 425-6266. Cantonese. $

Cornucopia on the Wharf, 101.
100 Atlantic Ave
☎ 367-0300. American. $$$$

Cottonwood Cafe, 45. 222 Berkeley St
☎ 247-2225. Southwestern. $$$

Daily Catch, 120. 323 Hanover St
☎ 523-8567. Seafood. $$

Dakota's, 68. 34 Summer St
☎ 737-1777. Steak. $$$

Davide, 110. 326 Commercial Ave
☎ 227-5745. Italian. $$$$

Davio's, 22. 269 Newbury St
☎ 262-4810. Italian. $$$

Domenico's, 97.
356 Bennington St, E Boston
☎ 567-8300. Italian. $$

Dom's, 130. 10 Bartlett Place
☎ 523-9279. Italian. $$$

Du Barry, 26. 159 Newbury St
☎ 262-2445. French. $$$

Durgin Park, 93. 340 Faneuil Hall Mktpl
☎ 227-2038. American. $$$

$$$$ = *over $35* $$$ = *$25–$35* $$ = *$15–$25* $ = *under $15*
Based on cost per person, excluding drinks, service, and 5% sales tax.

MAP **46** **Restaurants/Downtown**

Listed Alphabetically (cont.)

Emilio's, 114. 361 Hanover St
☎ 367-2246. Italian. $$

Emporio Armani Express, 23.
214 Newbury St
☎ 437-0909. Italian. $$$$

Enzo's, 3. 329 Harvard St, Brookline
☎ 277-1288. Italian. $$

Felicia's, 122. 145A Richmond St
☎ 523-9885. Italian. $$

Figs, 135. 67 Main St, Charlestown
☎ 242-2229. Pizza/Pasta. $

Filippo, 133. 283 Causeway
☎ 742-4143. Italian. $$

Five North Square, 107. 5 North Sq
☎ 720-1050. Italian. $$$

Florence's, 105. 190 North St
☎ 523-4480. Italian. $$

Galeria Umberto, 121. 289 Hanover St
☎ 523-9261. Italian. $

Giacomo's, 115. 355 Hanover St
☎ 523-9026. Italian. $$

Golden Palace, 61. 14 Tyler St
☎ 423-4565. Chinese. $$

Grill 23, 44. 161 Berkeley St
☎ 542-2255. Steak. $$$$

G'Vanni's, 117. 2 Prince St
☎ 523-0107. Italian. $$$

Gyuhama, 21. 827 Boylston St
☎ 437-0188. Japanese. $$$

Hamersley's Bistro, 39. 553 Tremont St
☎ 423-2700. Eclectic/French. $$$$

Hard Rock Cafe, 36. 131 Clarendon St
☎ 424-7625. American. $$

Ho Yuen Ting, 63. 13A Hudson St
☎ 426-2316. Chinese/Seafood. $$

House of Siam, 31. 21 Huntington Ave
☎ 267-1755. Thai. $$

Hungry I, 74. 71 1/2 Charles St
☎ 227-3524. American. $$$

Icarus, 43. 3 Appleton St
☎ 426-1790. American. $$$$

Il Panino, 126. 11 Parmenter St
☎ 720-1336. Italian. $$

Jacob Wirth, 57. 31 Stuart St
☎ 338-8586. German. $$

Jae's Cafe, 11. 520 Columbus Ave
☎ 421-9405. Korean. $$

Jasper's, 104. 240 Commercial St
☎ 523-1126. American. $$$$

Jimmy's Harborside, 87.
242 Northern Ave
☎ 423-1000. Seafood. $$$

Joseph's Aquarium, 100.
101 Atlantic Ave
☎ 523-4000. Seafood. $$$

Julien, 82.
Hotel Meridien, 250 Franklin St
☎ 451-1900. French. $$$$

King & I, 75. 145 Charles St
☎ 227-3320. Thai. $$

Kyoto, 49. 201 Stuart St
☎ 542-1166. Steak. $$$

La Summa, 109. 30 Fleet St
☎ 523-9503. Italian. $$

Legal Sea Foods, 48.
Park Plaza Hotel
☎ 426-4444. Seafood. $$$

L'Espalier, 17. 30 Gloucester St
☎ 262-3023. French. $$$$

**Library Grill at Hampshire
House, 85.** 84 Beacon St
☎ 227-9600. American. $$$

Locke-Ober Cafe, 69. 3 Winter Place
☎ 542-1340. American. $$$$

L'Osteria, 127. 109 Salem St
☎ 723-7847. Italian. $$

Maison Robert, 80. 45 School St
☎ 227-3370. French. $$$$

Mamma Maria, 106. 3 North Sq
☎ 523-0077. Italian. $$$$

Marais, 55. 116 Boylston St
☎ 482-7799. Eclectic. $$$

Massimino's, 132. 207 Endicott St
☎ 523-5959. Italian. $$

Mateo's, 116. 351 Hanover St
☎ 523-9265. Italian. $$

**Medieval Manor Theatre
Restaurant, 42.** 246 E Berkeley St
☎ 423-4900. Knightly Banquet. $$$

Michael's Waterfront, 102.
85 Atlantic Ave ☎ 367-6425.
Steak/Seafood. $$$

Mirabelle, 34. 85 Newbury St
☎ 859-4848. Nouvelle Cuisine. $$$

Mr Leung, 25. 545 Boylston St
☎ 236-4040. Chinese. $$$

Miyako, 20. 279A Newbury St
☎ 236-0222. Japanese. $$

Montien, 56. 63 Stuart St
☎ 367-2353. Thai. $$

Morton's of Chicago, 66. 1 Exeter Pl
☎ 266-5858. Steak. $$$$

Mother Anna's, 124. 211 Hanover St
☎ 523-8496. Italian. $$

MAP 46

Listed Alphabetically (cont.)

Nara, 83. 85 Wendell St
☎ 338-5395. Japanese/Korean. $$

Nicole, 128. 54 Salem St
☎ 712-6999 Italian. $$

No Name, 85. 15 1/2 Fish Pier
☎ 338-7539. Seafood. $$

Oasis Cafe, 131. 176 Endicott St
☎ 523-9274. American. $$

Olives, 134. 10 City Sq, Charlestown
☎ 242-1999. Italian. $$$

On the Park, 38. 315 Shawmut Ave
☎ 426-0862. American. $$

Papa Razzi, 28. 271 Dartmouth St
☎ 536-9200.
Italian/Mediterranean. $$$

Parker's, 78. Omni Parker House
☎ 227-8600. American. $$$$

Pho Pasteur, 58. 8 Kneeland St
☎ 451-0247. Vietnamese. $

Plaza Dining Room, 33.
Copley Plaza
☎ 267-5300. Continental. $$$$

Pushcart, 129. 61 Endicott St
☎ 523-9616. Italian. $$

Ristorante Lucia, 111. 415 Hanover St
☎ 367-2353. Italian. $$$

Ristorante Toscano, 72. 41 Charles St
☎ 723-4090. Italian. $$$

Rita's Place, 136. 88 Winnisimmet St,
Chelsea ☎ 884-9010. Italian. $$$

Ritz-Carlton Dining Room, 47.
15 Arlington St
☎ 536-5700. American. $$$

Rocco's, 54. 5 Charles St S
☎ 723-6800. Italian. $$$

Rowes Wharf Restaurant, 84.
Boston Harbor Hotel
☎ 439-3995. Seafood. $$$$

Sablone's, 96. 107A Porter St, E Boston
☎ 567-8140. Italian. $$$

St Cloud, 41. 557 Tremont St
☎ 353-0202. American. $$$

Sakura-bana, 88. 57 Broad St
☎ 542-4311. Japanese. $$

Saraceno's, 125. 286 Hanover St
☎ 227-5353. Sicilian. $$$

Sawasdee, 9.
320 Washington St, Brookline
☎ 566-0720. Thai. $$

Schifino, 89. 21 Broad St
☎ 523-0590. Italian. $$$

Scullers Grille, 2.
Guest Quarters Suite Hotel
☎ 783-0090. American. $$$

Seasons, 98. Bostonian Hotel
☎ 523-3600. American/Continental.
$$$$

Selaam, 12. 333 Mass Ave
☎ 424-1132. Ethiopian. $$

Siam Square, 59. 86 Harrison Ave
☎ 338-7706. Thai. $

Skipjack's, 35. 199 Clarendon St
☎ 536-3500. Seafood. $$$

Sol Azteca, 6.
914A Beacon St, Brookline
☎ 262-0909. Mexican. $$

Spasso, 27. 160 Commonwealth Ave
☎ 536-8656. Italian. $$$

Sports Depot, 1.
353 Cambridge St, Allston
☎ 783-2300. American. $$

Star of Siam, 50. 93 Church St
☎ 451-5236. Thai. $

Stars Ocean, 7. 70 Kilmarnock St
☎ 236-0161. Chinese. $

Tatsukichi, 90. 189 State St
☎ 720-2468. Japanese. $$$

Ten Huntington, 30. Westin Hotel
☎ 424-7429. Spanish. $$$

TGI Friday's, 24. 26 Exeter St
☎ 266-9040. American. $$

Thai Cuisine, 13. 14A Westland Ave
☎ 262-1485. Thai. $$

Turner Fisheries, 32. Westin Hotel,
10 Huntington Ave ☎ 424-742 $$$

29 Newbury, 29. 29 Newbury St
☎ 536-0290. American. $$

Union Oyster House, 99. 41 Union St
☎ 227-2750. Seafood/Raw Bar. $$

Veronique, 5. 20 Chapel St, Brookline
☎ 731-4800. French. $$$

Villa Francesca, 123. 150 Richmond St
☎ 367-2948. Italian. $$

Village Fish, 4.
22 Harvard St, Brookline
☎ 566-3474. Seafood. $$

Zumas Tex-Mex Cafe, 94.
Faneuil Hall Marketplace
☎ 367-9114. Tex-Mex. $$$

$$$$ = over $35 $$$ = $25–$35 $$ = $15–$25 $ = under $15
Based on cost per person, excluding drinks, service, and 5% sales tax.

MAP 47 **Restaurants/Cambridge**

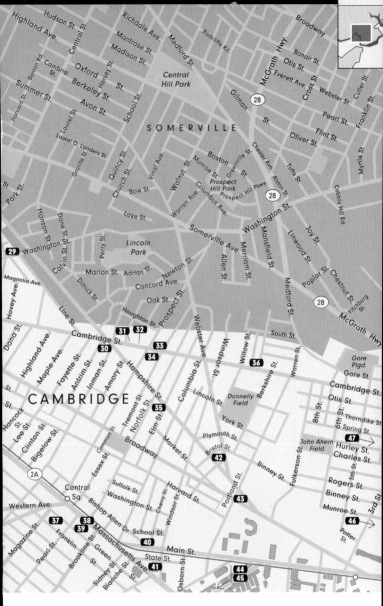

MAP **47**

MAP 47 **Restaurants/Cambridge**

Listed Alphabetically

Acropolis, 7. 1680 Mass Ave
☎ 492-0900.
Greek/American. $$

Anago Bistro, 41. 798 Main St
☎ 492-9500. American/European. $$$

Armadillo, 27. 1314 Commonwealth
Ave, Allston ☎ 232-4242. Tex/Mex. $$

Averof, 2. 1924 Mass Ave
☎ 354-4500. Greek/Middle Eastern. $$

Bisuteki, 28. 777 Memorial Drive
☎ 492-7777. Japanese/Steak. $$

Black Forest Cafe, 4. 1759 Mass Ave
☎ 661-6706. Stir-fry. $$

Blue Room, 42. 1 Kendall Square
☎ 494-9034. Mixed Ethnic. $$$

Boca Grande, 47. 149 First St
☎ 354-5550. Mexican. $

The Border Cafe, 14. 32 Church St
☎ 864-6100. Mexican/Cajun. $$

Cafe Sushi, 23. 1105 Mass Ave
☎ 492-0434. Japanese. $$

Cajun Yankee, 33. 1193 Cambridge St
☎ 576-1971. Cajun. $$

Casa Mexico, 18. 75 Winthrop St
☎ 491-4552. Mexican. $$

Casa Portugal, 34. 1200 Cambridge
St ☎ 491-8880. Portuguese. $$

Casablanca, 12. 40 Brattle St
☎ 876-0999. Seafood/Pasta. $$

Changsho, 5. 1712 Mass Ave
☎ 547-6565. Mandarin/Szechuan. $$

Chez Jean, 8. 1 Shepard St
☎ 354-8980. French. $$$

Chez Nous, 10. 147 Huron Ave
☎ 864-6670. French. $$$$

Daddy O's Bohemian Cafe, 35.
134 Hampshire St ☎ 354-8371. Eclectic. $

Dali, 29. 415 Washington St
☎ 661-3254. Spanish. $$$

East Coast Grill, 32. 1271 Cambridge
St ☎ 491-6568. BBQ/Caribbean. $$$

Goemon, 43. 1 Kendall Pl
☎ 577-9595. Japanese. $

Green St Grill, 39. 280 Green St
☎ 876-1655. Caribbean. $$

Grendel's Den, 16. 89 Winthrop St
☎ 491-1050. American. $$

Harvest, 13. 44 Brattle St
☎ 492-1115. American. $$$

India Pavilion, 37. 17 Central Sq
☎ 547-7463. Indian. $$

Iruna, 17. 56 JFK St
☎ 868-5633. Spanish. $$

John Harvard's Brew House, 19.
33 Dunster St ☎ 868-3585. American. $$

La Groceria, 40. 853 Main St
☎ 547-9258. Italian. $$

Little Osaka, 9. 465 Concord Ave
☎ 491-6600. Japanese. $$

Matsu-ya, 3. 1790 Mass Ave
☎ 491-5091. Japanese/Korean. $$

Mexican Cuisine, 6. 1682 Mass Ave
☎ 661-1634. Mexican. $$

Michela's, 46. 1 Athenaeum St
☎ 225-2121. Italian. $$$$

Mr Bartley's, 22. 1246 Mass Ave
☎ 354-6559. Burgers. $

New Korea, 31. 1281 Cambridge St
☎ 876-6182. Korean. $$

Pampas, 26. 928 Mass Ave
☎ 661-6613. Brazilian. $$

Peacock, 11. 5 Craigie Cir
☎ 661-4073. French. $$$

Porterhouse Cafe, 1. 2046 Mass Ave
☎ 354-9793. BBQ. $$

Rarities, 15. Charles Hotel
☎ 864-1200. American. $$$$

Roka, 24. 1001 Mass Ave
☎ 661-0344. Japanese. $$

S&S Deli, 30. 1334 Cambridge St
☎ 354-0620. Deli. $

Sally Ling's, 44. Hyatt Regency Hotel
☎ 868-1818. Chinese. $$$

Shalimar of India, 38. 546 Mass Ave
☎ 547-9280. Indian. $$

Spinnaker Italia, 45.
Hyatt Regency Hotel
☎ 492-1234. Italian. $$$

Sunset Cafe, 36. 851 Cambridge St
☎ 547-2938. Portuguese. $$

Tandoor House, 25. 991 Mass Ave
☎ 661-9001. Indian. $$

Upstairs at the Pudding, 21.
10 Holyoke St ☎ 864-1933.
Continental. $$$$

Wursthaus, 20. 4 JFK St ☎ 491-7110.
German. $$

$$$$ = over $35 $$$ = $25-$35 $$ = $15-$25 $ = under $15
Based on cost per person, excluding drinks, service, and 5% sales tax.

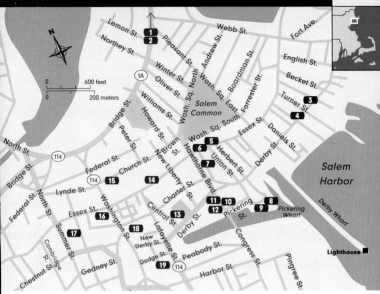

Listed by Site Number

1 Bridgeside	**8** Victoria Station	**15** Lyceum
2 Stromberg's	**9** Chase House	**16** Foodee's
3 Grand Turk Tavern	**10** Asahi	**17** Bambolino's
4 In a Pig's Eye	**11** Grapevine	**18** Lobster Shanty
5 Cafe de LaRosa	**12** Red Raven	**19** Dodge St Grill
6 Nathaniel's	**13** Roosevelt's	
7 Oh Calcutta	**14** Thai Place	

Listed Alphabetically

Asahi, 10. 21 Congress St
☎ 508/744-5376. Japanese. $$

Bambolino's, 17. 5 Summer St
☎ 508/741-1550. Italian. $$

Bridgeside, 1. 29 Bridge St
☎ 508/744-7777. American. $$

Cafe de LaRosa, 5. 107 Essex St
☎ 508/741-4088. Italian. $$$

Chase House, 9. Pickering Wharf
☎ 508/744-0000. Seafood. $$

Dodge St Grill, 19. 7 Dodge St
☎ 508/745-0139. American. $$

Grand Turk Tavern, 3. 110 Derby St
☎ 508/745-7727. Seafood/Amer. $$

Grapevine, 11. 26 Congress St
☎ 508/745-9335. American/Italian. $$

Foodee's, 16. 118 Washington St
☎ 508/740-9600. American. $$

In a Pig's Eye, 4. 148 Derby St
☎ 508/741-4436. American. $$

Lobster Shanty, 18.
Salem Marketplace ☎ 508/745-7449.
American. $$

Lyceum, 15. 43 Church St
☎ 508/745-7665. Continental. $$

Nathaniel's, 6. Hawthorne Inn Hotel
☎ 508/744-4080. American. $$$

Oh Calcutta, 7. 6 Hawthorne Blvd
☎ 508/744-6570. Indian. $$

Red Raven, 12. 75 Congress St
☎ 508/745-8558. Eclectic. $$

Roosevelt's, 13. 300 Derby St
☎ 508/745-9608. American. $$

Stromberg's, 2. 2 Bridge St
☎ 508/744-1863. Seafood/Amer. $$

Thai Place, 14. Museum Place Mall
☎ 508/741-8008. Thai. $$

Victoria Station, 8. Pickering Wharf
☎ 508/745-3400. American. $$

$$$$ = over $35 $$$ = $25-$35 $$ = $15-$25 $ = under $15
Based on cost per person, excluding drinks, service, and 5% sales tax.

MAP 49 Restaurants/Cape Ann

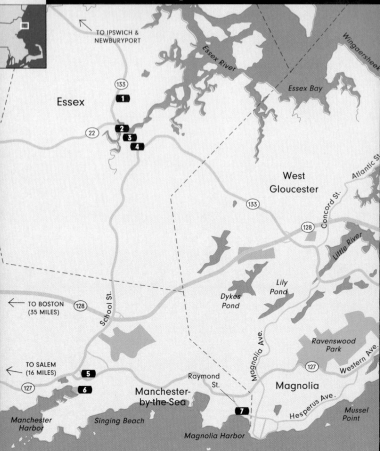

TO IPSWICH & NEWBURYPORT

Essex River

Essex Bay

Wingaersheek

133

1

Essex

22

2

3

4

West Gloucester

Atlantic St

133

Concord St

128

Little River

School St.

Lily Pond

Dykes Pond

Ravenswood Park

Western Ave.

TO BOSTON (128 MILES)

128

TO SALEM (16 MILES)

127

5

6

Manchester-by-the-Sea

Raymond St.

Magnolia Ave.

127

Magnolia

Hesperus Ave.

Mussel Point

Manchester Harbor

Singing Beach

7

Magnolia Harbor

Listed by Site Number

1	Woodman's	4	Tom Shea's
2	Max Callahan's	5	Seven Central
3	JP's Hearthside	6	Ben Sprague's

7	Edgewater Cafe
8	Rhumb Line
9	White Rainbow

Listed Alphabetically

Ben Sprague's, 6. 110 Beach St, Manchester
☎ 508/526-7168. Seafood. $$

Bistro, 13. 2 Main St, Gloucester
☎ 508/281-8055. Contemporary. $$$

Max Callahan's, 2. Main St, Essex
☎ 508/768-7750.
Seafood/American. $$

Cameron's, 10. 206 Main St, Gloucester ☎ 508/281-1331.
American. $$

Captain Courageous, 12.
25 Rogers St, Gloucester
☎ 508/283-0007. Seafood. $$

Edgewater Cafe, 7. 69 Raymond St, Manchester-by-the-Sea
☎ 508/526-4668. Mexican. $

Evie's Rudder, 11.
73 Rocky Neck, Gloucester
☎ 508/283-7697.
Seafood/Continental. $$

Greenery, 15. Dock Sq, Rockport
☎ 508/546-9593. Seafood. $$

The Gull, 14. 75 Essex St, Gloucester
☎ 508/283-6565. Seafood. $$

JP's Hearthside, 3. 109 Eastern Ave, Essex ☎ 508/768-6002.
Seafood/American. $$

MAP 49

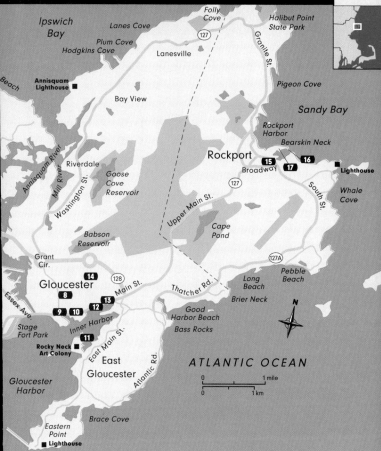

$$$$ = over $35 $$$ = $25-$35 $$ = $15-$25 $ = under $15
Based on cost per person, excluding drinks, service, and 5% sales tax.

MAP 50 Hotels/Greater Boston

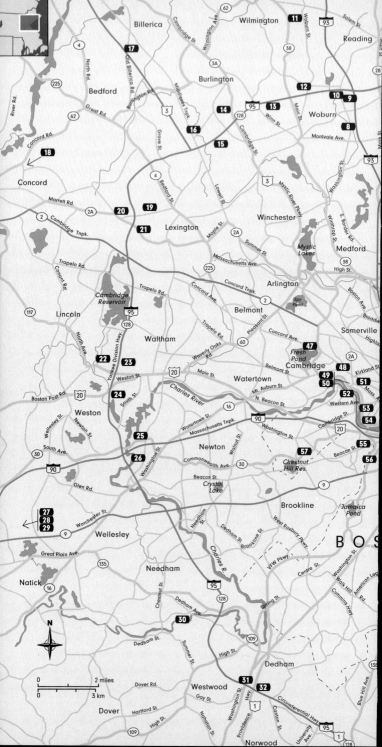

MAP 50

Lynnfield

Main St.

95

2

3

4

1

North St.

114

Summer St.

1

128

Main St.

Peabody

129

Lowell St.

6

Lynnfield St.

7

Salem St.

5

Water St.

129

Newburyport Tpke.

129

Lynnfield St.

Lynn St.

129

107

Salem

1A

Wakefield

Highland Ave.

Marblehead

Stoneham

Saugus

Main St.

Main St.

Paradise Rd.

Spot Pond

Wyoming Ave.

Lynn Fells Pkwy.

Hamilton Ave.

Lynn

Western Ave.

Swampscott

129

Highland Ave.

Upham St.

Melrose

1

44

43

107

Nahant Beach

Malden

Broadway

99

45

Nahant

Middlesex Ave.

60

60

1A

Lewis Beach

28

Main St.

1

Revere

Park Ave.

Broadway

Revere Beach

28

16

Everett

Revere Beach Pkwy.

ATLANTIC OCEAN

Northwest Expwy.

99

McClellan Hwy.

46

107

Chelsea

Bennington St.

145

28

1

42

Msgr. O'Brien Hwy.

93

1A

41

Winthrop

Winthrop Beach

Cambridge St.

40

Logan International Airport

Charles River

90

Summer St.

Huntington Ave.

Washington St.

1

D St.

Deer Island

93

3

E. Broadway

39

Dudley St.

Old Harbor

Long Island

Warren St.

Columbia Rd.

Thompson Island

Dorchester Ave.

38

Dorchester Bay

Moon Island

TON

Blue Hill Ave.

Talbot Ave.

Gallivan Blvd.

203

Quincy Shore Dr.

Nantasket Ave.

Brook Rd.

3A

Adams St.

Hull

Centre St.

37

Quincy

Sea St.

93

Adams St.

3

3A

Milton

Centre St.

28

3

53

Quincy Ave.

North St.

Hingham

33

Administration Rd.

36

Braintree

Weymouth

228

35

34

128

3

High St.

MAP **50** **Hotels/Greater Boston**

Listed by Site Number

1 King's Grant Inn
2 EconoLodge
3 Marriott Peabody
4 Sheraton Tower
5 Holiday Inn
6 Hilton Colonial
7 Best Western Lord Wakefield
8 HoJo Woburn
9 Radisson Woburn
10 Comfort Inn Woburn
11 Days Inn Woburn
12 Courtyard Marriott Woburn
13 Ramada Woburn
14 Marriott Burlington
15 Days Inn Burlington
16 HoJo Burlington
17 Stouffers Bedford Glen
18 HoJo Concord
19 Travelodge

20 Sheraton Lexington
21 Battle Green Inn
22 Guest Quarters Waltham
23 Best Western East
24 Westin Waltham
25 Marriott Newton
26 Days Inn Newton
27 Holiday Inn Crown Plaza
28 Travelodge Natick
29 Sheraton Tara
30 Inn on the Square
31 Holiday Inn
32 Comfort Inn Dedham
33 Holiday Inn
34 Sheraton Tara
35 HoJo Quincy
36 Days Inn Braintree
37 Quincy Bay Inn
38 Suisse Chalets
39 South Bay Hotel
40 Harborside Hyatt

41 Logan Airport Hilton
42 Ramada Airport
43 HoJo Revere
44 Days Inn Saugus
45 Town Line Inn
46 Holiday Inn
47 Best Western Homestead
48 Sheraton Commander
49 Charles Hotel
50 Harvard Manor House
51 Inn at Harvard
52 Guest Quarters Suite Hotel
53 Ho Jo Cambridge
54 Hyatt Regency
55 Holiday Inn
56 Best Western Inn at Children's
57 Best Western Terrace

Listed Alphabetically

Battle Green Inn, 21. 1720 Mass Ave, Lexington ☎ 862-6100. $

Best Western East, 23. 477 Totten Pd Rd, Waltham ☎ 890-7800. 📠 890-4937. $

Best Western Homestead, 47. 220 Alewife Pkwy, Cambridge ☎ 491-1890. 📠 491-4932. $$

Best Western Inn at Children's, 56. 342 Longwood Ave ☎ 731-4700. 📠 731-6273. $$

Best Western Lord Wakefield, 7. 595 North Ave, Wakefield ☎ 245-6100. 📠 245-2904. $

Best Western Terrace Motor Lodge, 57. 1650 Commonwealth Ave, Brighton ☎ 566-6260. 📠 731-3543. $

Charles Hotel, 49. 1 Bennett Sq, Cambridge ☎ 864-1200. 📠 864-5715. $$$

Comfort Inn Dedham, 32. 235 Elm St, Dedham ☎ 326-6700. 📠 326-9264. $

Comfort Inn Woburn, 10. 315 Mishawum Rd, Woburn ☎ 935-7666. 📠 933-6899. $

Courtyard Marriott Woburn, 12. 240 Mishawum Rd, Woburn ☎ 932-3200. 📠 935-6163. $$

Days Inn Braintree, 36. 190 Wood Rd, Braintree ☎ 848-1260. 📠 848-9799. $

Days Inn Burlington, 15. Wheeler Rd, Burlington ☎ 272-8800. 📠 270-9834. $

Days Inn Newton, 26. 399 Grove St, Newton ☎ 969-5300. 📠 965-4250. $

Days Inn Saugus, 44. Rt 1, Saugus ☎ 233-1800. 📠 233-1814. $

Days Inn Woburn, 11. 19 Commerce Way, Woburn ☎ 935-7110. 📠 932-0657. $$

EconoLodge, 2. 50 Dayton St, Danvers ☎ 508/777-1700. 📠 777-4647. $

Guest Quarters Suite Hotel, 52. 400 Soldiers Field Rd ☎ 783-0090. 📠 783-0897. $$$

Guest Quarters Waltham, 22. 550 Winter St, Waltham ☎ 890-6767. 📠 890-9097. $$$

Harborside Hyatt, 40. 101 Harborside Dr, Logan Airport ☎ 568-1234. 📠 374-9817. $$$$

Harvard Manor House, 50. 110 Mt Auburn St, Cambridge ☎ 864-5200. 📠 864-2409. $$

Hilton Colonial, 6. Rt 128, Wakefield

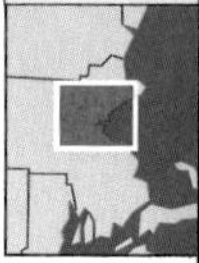

MAP 50

Listed Alphabetically (cont.)

☎ 245-9300. 🖷 245-0842. $$$

Holiday Inn, 55. 1200 Beacon St, Brookline ☎ 277-1200. 🖷 734-6991. $$

Holiday Inn Crown Plaza, 27. 1360 Worcester Rd, Natick ☎ 508/653-8800. 🖷 653-1708. $$$

Holiday Inn, 31. Rts 1 & 128, Dedham ☎ 329-1000. 🖷 329-0903. $$

Holiday Inn, 5. Rt 1, Peabody ☎ 508/535-4600. 🖷 535-8238. $$

Holiday Inn, 33. 1374 N Main St, Randolph ☎ 961-1000. 🖷 963-0089. $

Holiday Inn, 46. 30 Washington St, Somerville ☎ 628-1000. 🖷 628-0143. $$$

Howard Johnson's Burlington, 16. Rt 128, Burlington ☎ 272-6550. 🖷 229-8164. $

Howard Johnson's Cambridge, 53. 777 Memorial Dr, Cambridge ☎ 492-7777. 🖷 492-6038. $$$

Howard Johnson's Concord, 18. 740 Elm St, Concord ☎ 508/369-6100. 🖷 371-1656. $

Howard Johnson's Quincy, 35. 150 Granite St, Braintree ☎ 848-8500. 🖷 843-8389. $

Howard Johnson's Revere, 43. 407 Squire Rd, Revere ☎ 284-7200. 🖷 239-3176. $

Howard Johnson's Woburn, 8. Montvale Ave, Woburn ☎ 935-8160. 🖷 932-9623. $

Hyatt Regency, 54. 575 Memorial Dr, Cambridge ☎ 492-1234. 🖷 491-6906. $$$$

Inn at Harvard, 51. 1201 Mass Ave, Cambridge ☎ 491-2222. 🖷 491-6520. $$$

Inn on the Square, 30. 576 Washington St, Wellesley ☎ 235-0180. 🖷 235-5263. $$

King's Grant Inn, 1. Rt 128, Danvers ☎ 508/774-6800. 🖷 774-6502. $$$

Logan Airport Hilton, 41. Logan Airport ☎ 569-9300. 🖷 569-3981. $$$

Marriott Burlington, 14. Rts 128 & 3A, Burlington ☎ 229-6565. 🖷 229-7973. $$$

Marriott Newton, 25. Commonwealth Ave, Newton ☎ 969-1000. 🖷 527-6914. $$$

Marriott Peabody, 3. Rt 128, Peabody ☎ 508/977-9700. 🖷 977-0297. $$

Quincy Bay Inn, 37. 29 Hancock St, Quincy ☎ 328-1500. 🖷 328-3067. $

Radisson Woburn, 9. 2 Forbes Rd, Woburn ☎ 932-0999. 🖷 932-0903. $$$

Ramada Airport, 42. Rt 1A, E Boston ☎ 569-5250. 🖷 569-5159. $$

Ramada Woburn, 13. Rts 38 & 128, Woburn ☎ 935-8760. 🖷 938-1790. $

Sheraton Commander, 48. 16 Garden St, Cambridge ☎ 547-4800. 🖷 868-8322. $$$

Sheraton Lexington, 20. 727 Marrett Rd, Lexington ☎ 862-8700. 🖷 863-0404. $$$

Sheraton Tara, 34. 37 Forbes St, Braintree ☎ 848-0600. 🖷 843-9492. $$$

Sheraton Tara, 29. 1657 Worcester Rd, Framingham ☎ 508/879-7200. 🖷 875-7593. $$$

Sheraton Tower, 4. Ferncroft Rd, Danvers ☎ 508/777-2500. 🖷 777-2743. $$$

South Bay Hotel, 39. 5 Howard Johnson Plaza, Dorchester ☎ 288-3030. 🖷 265-6543. $

Stouffers Bedford Glen, 17. 44 Middlesex Tnpk, Bedford ☎ 275-5500. 🖷 275-8956. $$$

Susse Chalets, 38. 800 & 900 Morrissey Blvd ☎ 287-9100, 287-9200. 🖷 265-9287, 282-2365. $

Town Line Inn, 45. Rt 1, Malden ☎ 324-7400. 🖷 397-8501. $$

Travelodge, 19. 440 Bedford St, Lexington ☎ 861-0850. 🖷 861-0821. $

Travelodge Natick, 28. 1350 Worcester Rd, Natick ☎ 508/655-2222. 🖷 655-7953. $

Westin Waltham, 24. 70 Third Ave, Waltham ☎ 290-5600. 🖷 290-5626. $$$

$$$$ *= over $190* **$$$** *= $130-$190* **$$** *= $100-$130* **$** *= under $100*
Prices are for a standard double room, excluding 9.7% room tax.

MAP 51 Hotels/Downtown

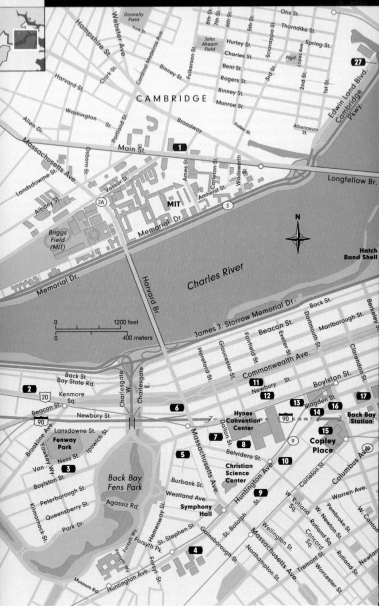

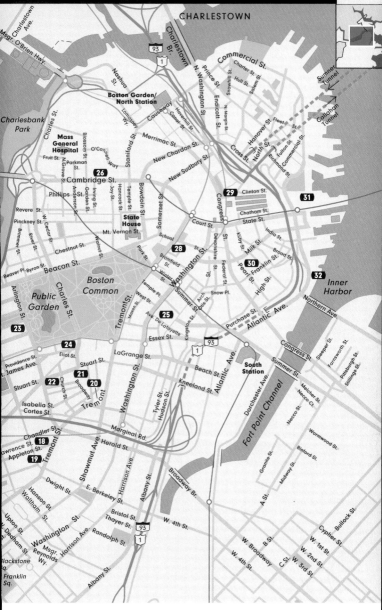

MAP 51

CHARLESTOWN

Boston Garden/
North Station

Charlesbank
Park

Mass
General
Hospital

Cambridge St.

State
House

Boston
Common

Public
Garden

South
Station

Inner
Harbor

Fort Point Channel

Listed by Site Number (cont.)

MAP 51 Hotels/Downtown

Listed Alphabetically

Back Bay Hilton, 7.
40 Dalton St
☎ 236-1100. ℻ 267-8893. $$$

Beacon Inns & Guesthouses, 12.
248 Newbury St
☎ 266-7142. ℻ 266-7276. $

Berkeley Residence Club (Women), 19. 40 Berkeley St
☎ 482-8850. $

Boston Harbor Hotel, 32.
70 Rowes Wharf
☎ 439-7000. ℻ 330-9450. $$$$

Boston International Hostel, 5.
12 Hemenway St ☎ 536-9455. $

Boston Park Plaza Hotel & Towers, 22. 64 Arlington St
☎ 426-2000. ℻ 423-1708. $$

The Bostonian, 29.
Faneuil Hall Marketplace
☎ 523-3600. ℻ 523-2454. $$$$

Cambridge Center Marriott, 1.
2 Cambridge Center
☎ 494-6600. ℻ 494-0036. $$$

Chandler Inn Hotel, 18.
26 Chandler St ☎ 482-3450. $

The Colonnade, 10.
120 Huntington Ave
☎ 424-7000. ℻ 424-1717. $$

Copley Plaza, 17. Copley Sq
☎ 267-5300. ℻ 267-7668. $$$$

Copley Square, 14.
47 Huntington Ave
☎ 536-9000. ℻ 267-3547. $$

Eliot Hotel, 6.
370 Commonwealth Ave
☎ 267-1607. ℻ 536-9114. $$

57 Park Plaza/Howard Johnson, 21.
200 Stuart St ☎ 482-1800. $$

Four Seasons, 24. 200 Boylston St
☎ 338-4400. ℻ 423-0154. $$$$

Greater Boston YMCA, 4.
316 Huntington Ave ☎ 536-7800. $

Holiday Inn-Government Center, 26. 5 Blossom St
☎ 742-7630. ℻ 742-7804. $$

Howard Johnson's Fenway, 3.
1271 Boylston St
☎ 267-8300. ℻ 267-2763. $$

Howard Johnson's Kenmore Sq, 2.
575 Commonwealth Ave
☎ 267-3100. ℻ 262-2959. $$

Le Meridien, 30. 250 Franklin St
☎ 451-1900. ℻ 423-2844. $$$$

Lenox Hotel, 13. 710 Boylston St
☎ 536-5300. ℻ 267-1237. $$$$

Marriott Copley Place, 15.
110 Huntington Ave
☎ 236-5800. ℻ 236-5885. $$$

Marriott Long Wharf, 31. 296 State St
☎ 227-0800. ℻ 227-2867. $$$

MidTown Hotel, 9.
220 Huntington Ave
☎ 262-1000. ℻ 262-8739. $$

Newbury Guest House, 11.
261 Newbury St
☎ 437-7666. ℻ 262-4243. $

Omni Parker House, 28. 60 School St
☎ 227-8600. ℻ 742-5729. $$$

Ritz-Carlton, 23. 15 Arlington St
☎ 536-5700. ℻ 536-1335. $$$$

Royal Sonesta, 27.
5 Cambridge Pkwy
☎ 491-3600. ℻ 661-5956. $$$

Sheraton Boston Hotel & Towers, 8.
39 Dalton St
☎ 236-2000. ℻ 236-1702. $$$

Swissôtel, 25. 1 Ave de Lafayette
☎ 451-2600. ℻ 451-0054. $$$$

Tremont House, 20. 275 Tremont St
☎ 426-1400. ℻ 482-6730. $$

Westin, 16. 10 Huntington Ave
☎ 262-9600. ℻ 424-7483. $$$$

$$$$ = over $190 $$$ = $130–$190 $$ = $100–$130 $ = under $100
Prices are for a standard double room, excluding 9.7% room tax.

Listed by Site Number

1 New School of Music
2 American Repertory Theatre/Loeb Drama Center
3 Longy Sch of Music
4 Sanders Theater
5 Hasty Pudding Theatre
6 Back Alley Theatre
7 Dance Umbrella
8 Little Flags Theatre
9 Kresge Auditorium
10 Cambridge Multicultural Arts Center

Listed Alphabetically

American Rep Theatre/Loeb Drama Center, 2. 64 Brattle St ☎ 547-8300

Back Alley Theatre, 6. I253 Cambridge St ☎ 576-I253

Cambridge Multicultural Arts Center, 10. 4I Second St ☎ 577-I400

Dance Umbrella, 7. 380 Green St ☎ 492-7578

Hasty Pudding Theatre/Harvard, 6. I2 Holyoke St ☎ 495-8400

Kresge Auditorium/MIT, 9. 77 Mass Ave ☎ 253-3913

Little Flags Theatre, 8. 550 Mass Ave ☎ 576-2800

Longy School of Music, 3. 27 Garden St ☎ 876-0956

New School of Music, 1. 25 Lowell St ☎ 492-8105

Sanders Theater/Harvard, 4. Quincy St ☎ 496-2222

MAP **53** **Performing Arts/Downtown**

MAP 53

MAP 54 **Movies/Boston Area**

ARLINGTON

MEDFORD

Concord Tnpk.

Broadway

Spy Pond

Prospect St.

Concord Ave.

BELMONT

Concord Ave.

Rindge Ave.

Blanchard Rd.

Alewife Brook Pkwy.

Porter Sq.

Mill St.

Pleasant St.

Common St.

Fresh Pond

Concord Ave.

2A

Massachusetts Ave.

Trapelo Rd.

School St.

Huron Ave.

Huron Ave.

Fresh Pond Pkwy.

Brattle St.

Garden St.

Harvard Sq.

Belmont St.

Arlington St.

Aberdeen Ave.

Mt. Auburn St.

Waverly Ave.

Common St.

WATERTOWN

School St.

Grove St.

JFK St.

Main St.

Mt. Auburn St.

Arsenal St.

Soldiers Field Rd.

N. Harvard St.

Western Ave.

River St.

Massachusetts Tnpk.

N. Beacon St.

Market St.

Cambridge St.

Brighton Ave.

Commonwealth Ave.

Centre St.

Washington St.

Chandler Pond

Harvard Ave.

Harvard St.

St. Paul St.

Lake St.

Chestnut Hill Ave.

Commonwealth Ave.

Beacon St.

NEWTON

Commonwealth Ave.

Cleveland Circle

Chestnut Hill Res.

Beacon St.

Boylston St.

Centre St.

Hammond Pond Pkwy.

Beacon St.

Langley Rd.

Hammond's Pond

Boylston St.

Brookline Reservoir

BROOKLINE

Listed by Site Number

MAP 54

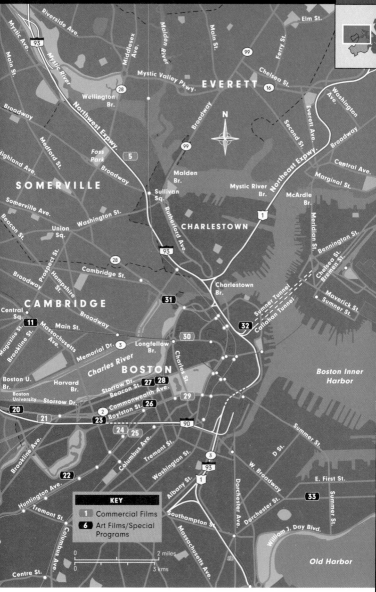

KEY

1 Commercial Films
6 Art Films/Special Programs

0 ——— 2 miles
0 ——— 3 kms

MAP 54 **Movies/Greater Boston**

KEY
34 Commercial Films
42 Art Films/Special Programs

Listed Alphabetically

COMMERCIAL FILMS

Allston Cinemas, 17. 214 Harvard Ave
☎ 277-2140

Arlington Capitol Cinema, 1.
204 Mass Ave ☎ 648-4340

Belmont Studio Cinema, 2.
376 Trapelo Rd ☎ 484-1706

**Braintree So Shore Plaza Cinemas
I–IV, 47.** So Shore Plaza ☎ 848-1070

Brattle Theater, 7. Brattle St,
Cambridge ☎ 876-6837

Brockton Loews Cinema, 49. Rt 27
☎ 963-1010

Charles Cinema 1–3, 30.
185 Cambridge St ☎ 222-1330

Cheri, 24. 50 Dalton St
☎ 536-2870

Chestnut Hill General Cinema, 15.
27 Boylston St ☎ 277-2500

Cinema 57, 29. 200 Stuart St
☎ 482-1222

Circle, 16. Cleveland Circle
☎ 566-4040

Coolidge Corner Cinema, 19.
Coolidge Corner, Brookline
☎ 734-2500

Copley Place, 25. 100 Huntington Ave
☎ 266-1300

Danvers Cinema City, 35. Rt 128
☎ 508/777-2555

Danvers Liberty Tree Mall, 34.
Liberty Tree Mall ☎ 508/777-1818

Dedham Community Cinemas, 43.
578 High St ☎ 326-1463

Dedham Showcase, 44. Rt 128
☎ 326-4955

Framingham General Cinema, 40.
Rt 9 Shoppers' World ☎ 508/872-4400

Fresh Pond Cinema, 3. Fresh Pond
Plz, Cambridge ☎ 661-2900

Harborlight Mall Cinema, 48.
Harborlight Mall, North Weymouth
☎ 864-4580

Harvard Square Theater, 8.
10 Church St, Cambridge ☎ 864-4580

Janus Theater, 10. 57 JFK St,
Cambridge ☎ 661-3737

Lexington Flick, 38. 1794 Mass Ave
☎ 861-6161

Natick Loews, 41. Rt 9
☎ 508/653-5005

Nickelodeon Loews, 21.
606 Commonwealth Ave ☎ 424-1500

**North Shore General
Cinema, 36.** Rt 128, Peabody
☎ 508/599-1310

Quincy Showcase, 46.
1585 Hancock St ☎ 773-5700

Revere Showcase, 39.
Rt 1 & Squire Rd ☎ 286-1660

Somerville Theater, 4. 55 Davis Sq
☎ 625-5700

Somerville Loews, 5.
Assembly Sq Mall ☎ 628-7000

West Newton Cinema, 14.
1296 Washington St ☎ 964-6060

Woburn Showcase, 37. Rts 128 & 38
☎ 933-5330

ART FILMS/SPECIAL PROGRAMS

Boston Public Library, 26.
666 Boylston St ☎ 536-5400

Boston Univ/Sherman Union, 20.
771 Commonwealth Ave ☎ 353-2169

Brighton Branch Library, 13.
40 Academy Hill Rd ☎ 782-6032

Brookline Public Library, 18.
361 Washington St ☎ 730-2360

Central Sq Library, 11. 45 Pearl St,
Cambridge ☎ 498-9081

Codman Sq Library, 45.
690 Washington St, Dorchester
☎ 436-8214

French Library, 28. 53 Marlborough St
☎ 266-4351

Goethe Institute, 27. 170 Beacon St
☎ 262-6050

Harvard Film Archive, 9.
24 Quincy St, Cambridge ☎ 495-4700

Institute of Contemporary Art, 23.
955 Boylston St ☎ 266-5151

Mt Auburn Library, 6. 64 Aberdeen
Ave, Cambridge ☎ 498-9085

Museum of Fine Arts, 22.
465 Huntington Ave ☎ 267-9300

Museum of Science, 31.
Science Park ☎ 523-6664

Newton Free Library, 12.
414 Centre St, Newton Ctr ☎ 552-7145

North End Branch Library, 32.
25 Parmenter St ☎ 227-8135

South Boston Branch Library, 33.
646 E Broadway ☎ 268-0180

Wellesley Free Library, 42. 530
Washington St ☎ 431-7813

MAP 55 **Nightlife/Cambridge & Somerville**

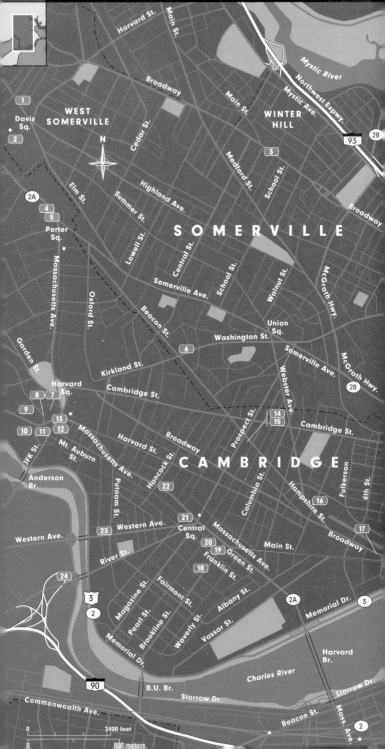

MAP 55

Listed by Site Number

1 Johnny D's
2 Somerville Theater
3 Willow
4 Averof
5 Toad
6 Nightgames
7 Passim
8 Black Rose
9 Cafe Algiers
10 Regattabar
11 House of Blues
12 John Harvard's Brew House
13 Wursthaus
14 Modern Times Cafe
15 Ryles
16 Kendall Cafe
17 Cambridge Brewing Co
18 Man Ray
19 TT The Bear's
20 Middle East
21 Cantab Lounge
22 Plough & Stars
23 Western Front
24 Scullers

Listed Alphabetically

Averof, 4. 1924 Mass Ave
☎ 354-4500. Greek/Middle Eastern Dancing

Black Rose, 8. 50 Church St
☎ 492-5740. Varied Music

Cafe Algiers, 9. 40 Brattle St
☎ 492-1557. Coffeehouse

Cambridge Brewing Co, 17.
1 Kendall Square
☎ 494-1994. Live Varied Music

Cantab Lounge, 21. 738 Mass Ave
☎ 354-2685. Live Rock/Blues

House of Blues, 11. 96 Winthrop St
☎ 491-2583. Blues

John Harvard's Brew House, 12.
33 Dunster St ☎ 868-3585.
Live Music/Bar

Johnny D's, 1. 17 Holland St
☎ 776-2004. Live Varied Music

Kendall Cafe, 16.
233 Cardinal Medeiros Way
☎ 661-0993. Live Acoustic Music

Man Ray, 18. 21 Brookline St
☎ 864-0400. Alternative

Middle East, 20. 472 Mass Ave
☎ 354-8238. Live Varied Music

Modern Times Cafe, 14.
134 Hampshire St ☎ 354-8371. Folk

Nightgames, 6. Holiday Inn,
30 Washington St
☎ 628-1000. DJ/Dancing

Passim, 7. 47 Palmer St
☎ 492-7679. Live Folk/Acoustic

Plough & Stars, 22. 912 Mass Ave
☎ 492-9653. Live Rock/Blues

Regattabar, 10.
Charles Hotel ☎ 864-1200. Live Jazz

Ryles, 15. 212 Hampshire St
☎ 876-9330. Live Jazz

Scullers, 24. Guest Quarters Suite Hotel, 400 Soldiers Field Rd, Allston
☎ 783-0811. Live Jazz

Somerville Theater, 2. Davis Sq
☎ 661-1250. Live Music

Toad, 5. 1912 Mass Ave
☎ 497-4950. Live Varied Music

T.T. The Bear's, 19. 10 Brookline St
☎ 492-2327. Live Music

Western Front, 23. 343 Western Ave
☎ 492-7772. Live Varied Music

Willow Jazz Club, 3. 699 Broadway
☎ 623-9874. Live Jazz

Wursthaus, 13. 4 JFK St
☎ 491-7110. Lounge

MAP **56** **Nightlife/Boston**

Kenmore Square & Lansdowne Street

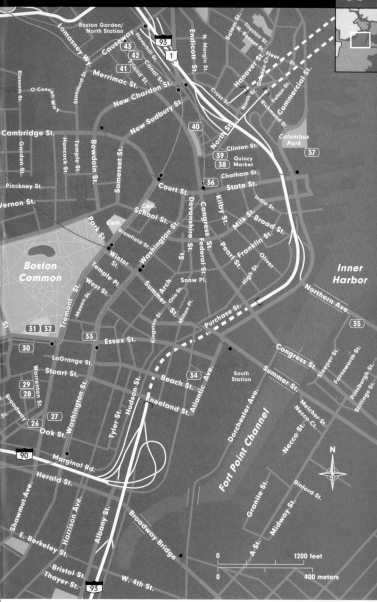

MAP **56**

MAP **56** Nightlife/Boston

Listed Alphabetically

Alley Cat, 30. I Boylston Place
☎ 351-2510. DJ

Avalon, 10. l5 Lansdowne St
☎ 262-2424. Dancing/Live Music

Avenue C, 31. l20 Boylston St
☎ 423-3832. New Wave

Axis, 9. l3 Lansdowne St
☎ 262-2424. Club/Varied Music

Bill's Bar, 7. 5 I/2 Lansdowne St
☎ 421-9595. Bar/Live Music

Boston Beach Club, 39.
300 Faneuil Hall Marketplace
☎ 227-9664. Top 40/Dancing

Boston Beer Works, 5.
6I Brookline Ave ☎ 536-2337. Brewery

Cask & Flagon, 2. 62 Brookline Ave
☎ 536-4840. Classic Rock

Cecil's, 34. l29 South St
☎ 542-5l08. Jazz/Folk

Chaps, 19. 27 Huntington Ave
☎ 266-7778. Dancing/Gay

Claddagh, 20. 335 Columbus Ave
☎ 262-9874. Live Music

Club Cafe, 22. 209 Columbus Ave
☎ 536-0966. Cabaret/Gay

Comedy Connection, 28.
76 Warrenton St
☎ 426-6339. Comedy

Commonwealth Brewing Co, 41.
138 Portland St ☎ 523-8383.
Brewery/Live Music

Copperfields, 1. 98 Brookline Ave
☎ 247-8605. Live Music

Daisy Buchanan's, 17.
240A Newbury St
☎ 247-8516. Bar/DJ

Diamond Jim's, 18. Lenox Hotel
☎ 421-4900. Piano/Singalongs/Jazz

Esme, 32. ll6 Boylston St
☎ 482-3399. DJ/Live Music

Frogg Lane, 38. Quincy Market
☎ 720-0610. Bar

Golf Club, 4. 3 Lansdowne St
☎ 262-0300. Indoor Mini-golf

Harp, 43. 85 Causeway St
☎ 742-1010. Rock/Dancing

Houlihan's, 36. 60 State St
☎ 367-6377. Dancing/DJ

Irish Embassy Pub, 42. 234 Friend St
☎ 742-6618. Live Music

Jake Ivory's, 3. I Lansdowne St
☎ 247-1222. Dueling Pianos

Jillians, 11. 145 Ipswich St
☎ 437-0300. Pool/Billiards

Jukebox/Galxc, 26. 275 Tremont St
☎ 542-1123. Dancing/DJ

Local 186, 12. 186 Harvard Ave,
Allston ☎ 351-2660. Rock/Reggae

Marketplace Cafe, 39.
300 Faneuil Hall Marketplace
☎ 227-9660. Live Music

Napoleon Club, 23. 52 Piedmont St
☎ 338-7547. Piano/Bar/Gay

Nick's Comedy Stop, 29.
l00 Warrenton St
☎ 482-0930. Comedy

Paradise, 13. 967 Commonwealth
Ave ☎ 351-2582. Live Music

Paramount, 31. 965 Mass Ave
☎ 523-8832. Varied Music/Dancing

Polly Esta's, 35. 145 Northern Ave
☎ 426-8600. Dancing/DJ

Purple Shamrock, 40. I Union St
☎ 227-2060. Bar/Varied Music

Quest, 14. l270 Boylston St
☎ 424-7747. Dancing/Gay/Straight

Rachel's, 37. Marriott Long Wharf
☎ 227-0800. Dancing/DJ

Rathskeller (The Rat), 6.
528 Commonwealth Ave
☎ 536-2750. Live Rock

Ritz-Carlton Bar, 24. 15 Arlington St
☎ 536-5700. Bar

The Roxy, 27. 279 Tremont St
☎ 338-7699. Live Music/Dancing

St Cloud, 21.
Tremont & Clarendon Sts
☎ 353-0202. Bar

Sticky Mike's, 33. 2I Boylston St
☎ 426-2583. Live Blues

Tia's, 37. Marriott Long Wharf
☎ 227-0828. Outdoor Bar

Venus de Milo, 8. ll Lansdowne St
☎ 421-9595. Live Music/Dancing

Zachary's, 16. Colonnade Hotel
☎ 424-7000. Live Jazz

Zanzibar, 30. I Boylston Place
☎ 351-7000. Dancing/DJ